COOPERATION ■ COMMITMENT

WATERSHED

The Watershed Whole-Learning Activities Book

by
Mark Springer

National Middle School Association
Columbus, Ohio

National Middle School Association
2600 Corporate Exchange Drive, Suite 370
Columbus, Ohio 43231
Telephone (800) 528-NMSA

Sue Swaim, Executive Director
Jeff Ward, Assistant Executive Director, Business Services
John Lounsbury, Senior Editor
Edward Brazee, Associate Editor
Mary Mitchell, Copy Editor/Designer
Marcia Meade, Senior Publications Representative
ISBN: 1-56090-156-X   NMSA Stock Number: 1253

Library of Congress Cataloging-in-Publication Data
Springer, Mark
    The Watershed whole-learning activities book/ by Mark Springer.
      p.   cm.
    ISBN: 1-56090-156-X
    1.Education--Experimental methods.   2. Interdisciplinary approach in education.   3. Language experience approach in education.
    4. Middle school education--Activity programs. I. Title
    373.139--dc21   98-29915
                                                   CIP

Contents

Acknowledgements

So many people helped make this book a reality that I run the real risk of forgetting someone important as I try to thank those who helped in any way. If such should prove the case, I beg forgiveness and plead insanity. The quality of the people who aided me in this venture assures me of the former; my own reputation takes care of the latter.

First and foremost, I owe the greatest debt to my teaching partner and collaborator, Ed Silcox, who has had an equal hand in developing all the activities and forms presented here. We have worked together so long and so well that the lines that separate our respective thoughts and our ideas have gone the way of the lines that separate academic disciplines. Truly Ed deserves a full measure of the credit for the success of WATERSHED and, by extension, of my writing about it.

A number of other special people have been instrumental in encouraging me and in helping me with this endeavor. Not the least among them are Wally Alexander, John Arnold, Ross Burkhardt, Kathy McAvoy, and Chris Stevenson; mentors all who have given me significant support and guidance.

No listing of contributors would be complete without mention of Mary Mitchell, Ed Brazee, and John Lounsbury at NMSA. Mary works tirelessly finding my errors and working out all the details of the layout and design. As my chief editor and mentor, John Lounsbury sits somewhere between heaven and earth. I am eternally in his debt for the wisdom, energy, and determination he continually expends on my behalf. Ed carried this project through to a successful conclusion, and I cannot adequately thank him for his dedication.

To my wife, Allison, and my children, Colin and Lauren, thanks for the time they sacrifice in allowing me to write can never be adequately expressed or repaid.

Finally, I want to thank all the students who have shaped and reshaped the WATERSHED program through its eleven year history. They are the ones who have tested and proved these activities. They are the ones who have shown day in and day out with their enthusiasm and their joy that whole-learning works. — *Mark Springer, July 1998*

The Philosophy Behind Whole Learning

1.

How do *you* **learn??** You do it all the time. Indeed, learning comes so naturally that most of us take it for granted. But think about *learning* for a moment; based on your own experiences as a learner, what do you really know about this most common of human activities?

For one thing, you know that when you are truly learning, you become so totally engaged in the learning activity that all "irrelevant" stimuli seem to vanish. You also know that this experience is very enjoyable. But how do you become so totally engrossed, and what makes the experience so pleasant? Just what constitutes a learning experience and what circumstances enhance it?

Just what constitutes a learning experience, and what circumstances enhance it?

Reflecting upon these questions, you'll discover that those moments when you are truly learning share several basic characteristics. For the sake of a quick analysis, let's explore three general segments of the learning experience we will call the *Initiation*, *Participation,* and *Application* phases.

Initiation

Every learning situation begins with a framework of meaning that determines motivation. Before learning can occur, a context must already exist. This context provides the significance for and the vested interest in the learning. For some reason, *you* decide the experience is one you need and want. Perhaps your curiosity is aroused; perhaps you are trying to accomplish an important task and realize you require some other information or skill in order to achieve your goal. The reason can be conscious or subconscious, overt or subtle, practical or whimsical; no matter. The important aspect common to all learning situations is that *you* determine that reason or need; *you* have the desire, the motivation to learn.

Furthermore, the chances are that motivation is a positive one. Your most memorable and successful learning moments most likely stem from

1

pleasurable experiences, not frightening, stressful, or painful ones. If the initiatory phase of the learning experience involves negative motivation, if your mind is dwelling on a threatened punishment, then the learning experience will be a negative one with less than adequate results. The old adage, *you catch more bees with honey than with vinegar*, holds true for learning. You learn best when the experience is enjoyable, and this starts with the motivation behind the experience.

You learn best when the experience is enjoyable, and this starts with the motivation behind the experience.

This brings us back to the other aspect of motivation. As pleasure is a highly personalized experience, so is learning. No one can ever truly determine the motivation for someone else. We can suggest. We can offer arguments or incentives. We can even try to coerce. But, ultimately, the motivation lies with *you*, the learner. You will learn best when and if you want to learn. It stands to reason, however, that you will tend to want to learn more when the circumstances are pleasant and fulfilling.

This, of course, is one of your primary roles as a teacher. We spend a great deal of time and energy trying to motivate our students, trying to convince or cajole them into believing they should want to learn what we want to teach. Indeed, that is ultimately what this book is about. For the moment, however, let's continue our general analysis of learning experiences by moving from the initiation phase to the second phase, participation.

Participation

Once a learner has a reason and a desire to learn something, the actual learning phase begins. This is the phase we recognized previously, characterized by total involvement. Involvement is generated and maintained through a combination of three factors.

First, there is the *personal sense of control*. This starts with the original context and motivation to learn, and it continues throughout the learning experience. You are in control because you recognized the need to learn and made the decision to satisfy that need. If this sense of control dissipates for any reason, the depth of the learning experience decreases significantly, perhaps even to the point where the learning ceases altogether. This is one of many reasons why force or threatened punishment does not promote learning. These methods can produce a conditioned response. However, I contend that such responses do not constitute true learning because they lack this necessary component of learner control. When the learner feels in control of the motivation, then he or she feels the vested interest needed to engage and focus the fullest levels of attention.

Second, as implied above, the *depth of motivation* then determines the degree to which each of the learner's senses and mental faculties is engaged and focused on the experience. This is why all stimuli outside the learning context seem to vanish during moments of real learning.

These first two factors then generate the third, which is *pleasure*. You are in control, and you are using all your brain's assets to satisfy a need that is meaningful to you. As your mind fulfills its cognitive function, you gain a definite sense of enjoyment from the process of learning. In short, true learning then becomes fun.

In short, true learning is fun.

Application

The third phase of the learning experience is *application*. This phase is characterized by the self-awareness that the learning has been accomplished and can now be applied. You experience a sense of satisfaction because you have filled the need established in the initiation phase. Along with this sense of satisfaction often comes a feeling of pride. Because the need was yours, the control was yours, and the effort was yours, you now deserve the credit for a job well done. Obviously the extent of this pride depends in part on the degree of difficulty inherent in the learning task itself and on the level of significance assigned to the task in the initiatory phase. Nevertheless, true learning usually yields some sense of pride, a confirmation of your abilities to achieve a goal; this is a pleasurable feeling that rounds out the enjoyment derived from a true learning experience.

So the general characteristics of a true learning experience are:

- a self-determined, highly personalized context which constitutes the motivation to learn
- an ongoing sense of personal control over the experience
- the opportunity to engage many of your senses and abilities
- a sense of enjoyment throughout the experience
- an awareness of achievement and potential application

These five characteristics, though highly simplified here, are necessary in every real learning experience. The extent to which each is optimized determines the overall success of the learning. If any one of these is missing or significantly curtailed, the learning is jeopardized and perhaps aborted altogether.

None of this is particularly radical or even new. We all know that we learn best when the learning objective is of special interest and relevance to us. We have all experienced the joy of true learning experiences, those

We have all experienced the joy of true learning experiences, those moments when all five of the characteristics have come together. The results are almost magical.

moments when all five of the characteristics have come together. The results are almost magical.

Now as a teacher, ask yourself how often do we apply this knowledge of how *we* learn to our students and to our curricular planning? How often do the students have the opportunity to enjoy learning activities that encompass all the characteristics we have listed? Ask students, and you'll find the answer is "seldom." No wonder so many students find school stifling and boring.

Intentional? Certainly not. Teachers do not choose this career field in order to frustrate students or to impede the learning process. Why, then, do we so often do just that? The answer is complex, varying from teacher to teacher and school to school, but it involves several key points.

First, the educational system as it currently exists ignores the essential nature of learning just described. The system is subject/content-centered, not learner-centered. As a result, students in most traditional situations do not have the chance to develop any vested interest in the subjects at hand: they do not choose to be in a given class or to study a given topic. Even in high schools where students appear to have a choice of courses, those choices are limited, masking curricular requirements. The student who has no vested interest in biology, for example, is allowed to select from biology courses with varying degrees of complexity, but still must take a biology course. We all know the routine. Most of us simply resigned ourselves and suffered through a myriad of courses with no apparent relevance to our lives. We were frequently bored to death, and it is doubtful whether much true learning occurred in those situations. In essence, we wasted a lot of valuable learning time and energy insuring that we "passed" courses; then we promptly forgot most of what we had encountered. We believed, as most people continue to believe, that there is no alternative. This is what school is all about, and we must endure it.

We need a system of education that promotes true learning by encouraging self-determined learning contexts, ones that foster students' control over their own learning initiatives.

As we become teachers, we forget how much we disliked this situation, and we become agents in perpetuating it. Clearly, we need to develop a strategy that incorporates fully all five characteristics of the learning process. We need a system of education that promotes true learning by encouraging self-determined learning contexts, ones that foster students' control over their own learning initiatives.

I can hear the counter argument coming. Critics will claim: *Children don't know enough to decide what they need to learn; therefore, as adults we have to make those decisions for them.*

4

Interestingly, children begin learning at birth. They have made learning decisions for years before they enter school. Most learn a language long before they set foot in a classroom, and that learning involves incredibly complex concepts, relationships, and symbols. Similarly, thousands of generations of humans have managed to push forward the boundaries of human understanding without the benefit of institutionalized intervention. To defend current teaching practices on the basis of children's inability to learn any other way is patently ridiculous.

Still, the teacher in the back row will contest: *Then tell me why when I give my seventh graders the chance to choose a topic for themselves, they often seem confused and the resulting projects are dismal failures.*

I see two reasons for this, both stemming from the system of education, not from any lack of ability on the child's part. First, from kindergarten on the system, i.e. *school,* teaches children NOT to think for themselves. The very structure of the classroom demands a certain uniformity of experience which inhibits or precludes the first two characteristics of a true learning situation. Students are restricted from following their self-determined and highly personalized contexts that constitute the motivation to learn; and they lose control over the experience. We teach the children to ignore their inherent ability to establish contexts and motivation for learning and instead to accept *our* reasons for every learning experience. Through the classroom system of punishments and rewards, the child quickly discovers that "success" and sometimes even survival are measured in terms of conformity. It becomes less painful (with respect to punishment) and perhaps more pleasureable (with respect to rewards) to follow the teacher's directions than to follow one's self-determined learning contexts. The child is thus socialized into the culture of *school,* but he or she is simultaneously distanced from the natural process of true learning.

Second, when we do give students choices, the options are false or limited. The students frequently have no vested interest in the task, no self-determined context, no motivation. In short, the very choice we allow may not be relevant to the students.

With these two strong factors working against us, it is little wonder that when a teacher sincerely tries to allow students some freedom to direct their own learning, the students react with hesitation, confusion, and skepticism. Though this is certainly not a new concept, it bears repeating: *we would save time, energy, and pain, and students would learn more if we concentrated from the very beginning of the school experience on what students want to learn and when the students want to learn it.*

Another major factor preventing us from adequately fostering the learning process is the institutionalized perception of the teacher's role. Many teachers continue to see that role as one of dispensing knowledge; a role that at first appears to make sense in light of our discussion of the learning process. After all, the teacher has a personal interest in a particular topic or subject area. The teacher wants to share the enjoyment he or she has gained from pursuing that interest. So far this fits perfectly with our understanding of the learning process. Unfortunately, the teacher often overlooks the extent to which his or her personal interest and the self-directed act of discovery originally affected that sense of pleasure and accomplishment. As a result, the teacher mistakenly presumes that he or she can transfer those feelings to the students along with subject information. Yet, the teacher, in merely dispensing information, limits the students' active participation in the learning situation and precludes the students' self-directed acts of discovery that lie at the heart of learning. Teaching in this manner, and it has been the traditionally recognized norm, the institutionalized method perpetuated in most teacher training programs threatens the very process it is supposed to enhance.

How then can we work within this system, inherently flawed as it is, to maximize the opportunities our students get to enjoy true learning experiences? Clearly, the answer lies in creating curricular structures and activities that incorporate all five characteristics of the learning experience and, at the same time, redefine the role of the teacher. Fortunately, these two tasks go hand-in-hand quite naturally.

Clearly, the answer lies in creating curricular structures and activities that incorporate all five characteristics of the learning experience and, at the same time, redefine the role of the teacher.

Those who have read *WATERSHED: A Successful Voyage Into Integrative Learning* are already familiar with the philosophy of *whole-learning*. For those who may not be familiar with this philosophy, *whole-learning* is an alternative to traditional practices. In a whole-learning program students explore a thematic focus of their own choosing, based on their own interests. There are no separate classes in the traditional academic disciplines. Rather, elements of those artificially segregated subject areas are reunified and focused on the central theme. All learning is cooperative, not competitive, and students have a great deal of control over their learning. Ideally, whole-learning programs are self-contained, as is WATERSHED, and they consist of relatively small groups. These characteristics allow for greater flexibility with respect to time and to the types of activities that can be developed – as the following chapters will demonstrate. These factors, coupled with students' shared sense of purpose, also help to create a learning community better equipped to meet the needs of each learner within the program. Finally, the program does not use grades or other negative inducements that impede several of the basic characteristics of true learning experiences. The focus is always on a positive environment in which students feel that they belong and are equal partners in the adventure we call education.

The whole-learning approach seeks to restructure the learning environment to more effectively promote the five characteristics of the learning process. Some would argue that any such restructuring is futile because students do not want to be in school to begin with, and that strips away all hope of self-determined learning. On one level I agree; but we must take a look at why students don't want to be in school. Is it because they don't want to learn? Clearly not. Learning, as we have seen, is a pleasurable activity all humans enjoy. I contend that students don't want to be in school because they recognize that the institution does not promote learning and, therefore, is not enjoyable. Learning and its concomitant pleasure can be more readily experienced anywhere but in school. If this is indeed the case, then a change in the structure of school could ultimately lead to a change in students' attitudes toward school. They could actually start to want to be there. Once that change occurs, the student again has the basic sense of control through self-determined motivation.

The whole-learning approach seeks to restructure the learning environment to more effectively promote the five characteristics of the learning process.

Can this change occur? I have personally seen it with countless WATERSHED students. Over the years we have documented numerous cases of students who hated coming to school in the years prior to their WATERSHED experience, but who began to look forward to school each day during their WATERSHED year. School became an enjoyable place, a place where they *wanted* to be. Returning to the traditional structure the following year, many students quickly came to dislike school once again. So, restructuring the system is not futile. Indeed, it is necessary.

How does a whole learning program such as WATERSHED restructure the approach to education?

The first and crucial step is to allow students choices and control over their learning. In WATERSHED, this begins by allowing students to decide whether or not the program is of interest to them (as you will see). Students retain this control throughout the activities.

The second important aspect is this central focus, itself. A whole-learning program discards traditional academic disciplines that tend to fragment experience into artificial categories. Learning is a constructive activity of pattern building, a synthetic process of converging order and meaning. A traditional curriculum of academic disciplines creates barriers that, while admittedly allowing synthesis within disciplines, disrupts the formation of the larger and more important relationships among these limited areas.

A whole-learning program discards traditional academic disciplines that tend to fragment experience into artificial categories.

7

In contrast, a whole-learning program selects a focus topic and examines it from the widest possible number of vantage points. Students are free to range over a world of knowledge and experiences looking for interrelationships with the topic focus. The students are encouraged to explore the methods and techniques of all the so-called disciplines without being limited to the exclusive use of any particular one.

This promotes the characteristics of a true learning experience on several levels. The students have control over numerous, real facets of the experience. They select the larger focus, then they continue to make decisions directing the course of their learning, because neither the group nor any individual is locked into a set curricular path that supersedes the needs and motivations of the learner.

This is not to say that the teacher relinquishes control over the learning environment. In fact, the special relationship between teacher and students in a whole-learning program actually gives the teacher more meaningful influence over learning opportunities. The type of control exerted, however, is different from that of a traditional program.

By shifting the emphasis away from distinct academic disciplines onto wider relationships, the need for separate classes dissipates as well. This, in turn, means that the daily schedule can be radically realigned for more effective use of time and resources. Without the need to change classes every forty minutes, students can spend a far longer period of time on the tasks they have selected. They can also be allowed far greater control over their use of this time. On both counts, along with this control students assume greater responsibility for their learning. Control and responsibility, as we have seen, comprise the necessary basics of a true learning process.

Similarly, students don't need to change teachers. A group of students can stay with the same teacher or teachers virtually all day. This provides a valuable continuity of experience without jeopardizing students' sense of participation in controlling their learning. Students and teachers get to know each other far better than can ever happen in a traditional structure. The advantages of such familiarity are obvious; teachers get to know students' strengths, weaknesses, and characteristic behaviors. This allows the teacher the chance to tailor opportunities to each child's learning style. This is the heightened level of influence mentioned earlier. This is not the traditionally direct control over content and method. It is rather the more significant cooperative influence a teacher can provide when he or she really knows the students and has the time to work closely with each one of them individually – luxuries not permitted by the traditional structure of most *school* situations.

These logistical changes of time and structure within the school day both demand and make possible relatively small class sizes. In a regular program of studies, eight or so teachers often share 100 to 200 students spread out over seven, eight, or nine forty-minute periods during the day. This scenario, common to many schools, leaves no time for any teacher to get to know most of the students or to work individually with them. The teacher cannot even read papers from all those students in a timely manner, lct alone make significant comments and suggestions on each student's work.

By contrast, the same number of students could be grouped in smaller learning communities which, because they share a common interest, remain with the same teacher, or at least fewer teachers, for the bulk of the day. The number of students involved in each community should be based on the extent to which the group can remain intact for activities. If the group continually needs to be subdivided and separated, then the group is too large. Our experience in WATERSHED has shown that a team of two teachers with about forty students works particularly well in light of the specific activities we employ. A different topic focus with different types of activities might allow for a slightly larger number of students. However, the more students the lower the amount and the quality of time teachers can devote to each child. This, in turn, limits the flexibility and the success of the learning experiences. Keep in mind that it is necessary for each teacher in the community to *get to know and to work individually* with each of the students. From personal experience, I contend that a learning community consisting of more than fifty students with a partner team of two teachers is unworkable. One should note, however, that limiting the number of students is not dramatically different from classroom teacher-student ratios in most schools. Entire schools could be restructured along whole learning lines without significantly increasing or decreasing the number of teachers required.

The added advantages of this altered structure are numerous. Aside from getting to know students better, teachers get to know parents better as well. The smaller class size and the greater time commitment permits greater and more meaningful communication with parents. In fact, it provides far more opportunities for parents to be directly involved in their children's education, as you will see in some of the later discussions of particular activities.

Similarly, this structure permits teachers time to review adequately each and every child's work and to provide meaningful feedback to help the student. A look at numbers tells the tale: If I have 120 students in a traditional program, each single essay assignment produces 120 papers for me to read, correct, and annotate. If I have forty students in a whole-learning community, 120 essays represents three samples, perhaps even improved drafts of the same essay from each student.

Furthermore, in a traditional format, the 120 essays often tend, by dictate of a preestablished curriculum, to come in almost simultaneously. This means many students have to wait days before receiving feedback. This delay can be costly. In a smaller whole-learning community with far fewer papers to handle on any given occasion, feedback is more immediate. In fact, the whole-learning structure sometimes permits papers to be returned on the very same day; this cannot happen when students turn in papers and then disappear to other teachers for the remainder of the day. The advantages this heightened level of feedback provides to the students' learning process are too obvious to delineate here.

Perhaps less obvious but equally important is the teacher's fatigue factor. As every teacher knows, it is sufficiently difficult to maintain a fresh perspective and make meaningful comments if you have to read forty similar essays or reports in a short period of time: it is virtually impossible to do so with 120. The whole-learning structure keeps the impact of this teacher fatigue factor to a minimum, which clearly helps both teacher and students.

An environment is created that enhances the learning process by promoting, right from the onset, the five basic characteristics of that process.

Summarizing thus far, a whole-learning program restructures the system by creating small communities of learners who have *elected* to spend a significant portion of their school time together exploring a focus *topic of interest* to them all. This community stays together with one or two teachers, does not change classes, and does not separate learning into academic disciplines. An environment is thus created that enhances the learning process by promoting, right from the onset, the five basic characteristics of that process.

How, then, are these basic characteristics of the learning experience further enhanced and fostered within the whole-learning environment?

Having established a fundamental interest through the choice of the focus topic, students have determined for themselves a context and have acquired a vested interest that promotes positive motivation. The task now is to maintain that positive motivation. Whole-learning programs do this in several ways. The first of these is by providing a non-threatening environment void of the negative motivational factors employed in most traditional systems, namely, forced peer competition and graded evaluation.

As you will see, all the activities described in this volume rely on cooperative learning strategies. The students are encouraged to work together, to share information and skills, and to rely on each other for the common good. After all, the group shares a common interest, the focus topic they all selected; so any information or skill relevant to that focus is of value to every member of the group and should be available to every member of the group. If there is a question or a problem concerning the focus topic, the entire group shares a vested interest in answering the question and solving the problem. In real world, real life situations, problem solving is best achieved through cooperation. Doctors consult with one another; so do lawyers, engineers, designers, sales personnel, and even teachers. Why should students' problem solving experiences be any different – particularly if we are supposed to be preparing the students to fill such cooperative roles in the real world beyond school?

Similarly, in the real world, people do not receive grades. Performance is evaluated in real ways based on results that are significant to a particular line of effort. A salesperson does not take a test on selling techniques and then get a grade. The salesperson is judged on how much he sells. A mechanic may take a test on the systems of an automobile, but the real test of that mechanic's abilities is whether the cars she worked on run well or not. I could go on and on. In a whole-learning classroom, performance evaluation is based on results of significance to the focus topic and is geared specifically toward the improvement of skills needed to ensure a successful outcome. In WATERSHED, for example, students don't take a test on water quality analysis techniques; they go to a stream and analyze the water. Their analysis will quickly reveal whether or not they have mastered the procedures. If they cannot adequately perform a procedure, that procedure is reviewed and practiced until the student can perform it successfully. No grade is attached to this process. Instead, the student and his/her family receive a narrative describing both the areas in which the student experiences difficulties and the steps the student can follow to overcome those difficulties.

Similarly, students don't take a test on how to write a letter; they write letters to all sorts of professionals. Each letter, however, is proofread and rewritten until it meets the necessary criteria, just as in the real world of business. With each draft suggestions are made by the teacher and by peers for ways the writer can improve the letter's mechanics and content. The cooperative performance review is ongoing and non-judgmental. The emphasis is on a continuum of progress rather than graded levels or plateaus.

As a result, students see their work and its evaluation as having direct application to their larger interest. This helps maintain positive motivation. Too often students are given learning tasks for which they see no immediate application. Such exercises fail on two levels: one, the task is assigned, not self-determined; and, two, it lacks significant application other than a grade. Little wonder such exercises generate little enthusiasm and poor results.

...self-evaluation maintains the integrity of the learner's control over the learning experience.

Furthermore, any evaluation in a whole-learning program should begin with a self-evaluation by the student. Once again, this mirrors the experience most will have outside of school where people continually evaluate their own performance and seek ways to improve. What is more, self-evaluation maintains the integrity of the learner's control over the learning experience. This validates the experience for students as they recognize that they, not the teacher, are ultimately responsible for their actions and their learning. Traditional programs where the teacher "gives" the student a grade subtly shifts that responsibility away from students and onto the teacher. No matter how often we try to tell our students that they "earn" their grades, they invariably see it differently, because our actions speak louder than our words.

So, whole-learning programs remove the negative motivation of grades as well as that of forced competition and replace them with positive motivators of performance outcome reviews, self-evaluation, and cooperative learning strategies.

Throughout the foregoing discussion, I have frequently commented on real world or real life experiences outside the classroom. This brings us to another major component of whole-learning. The program should emphasize real world/real work activities. Students need to recognize a direct connection between their scholastic efforts and activities in the real world. Too often that connection is blurred or lost entirely in traditional programs where a particular discipline, concept, or skill becomes an end unto itself rather than a stepping stone or a means to a more important goal. Isolated grammar exercises are a classic example of this phenomenon. Students plow through exercises in grammar textbooks, often lists of unrelated sentences or isolated paragraphs, but the motivation behind this effort has nothing to do with the learning task. The grammar is not of immediate use because the exercises themselves are of no use to the student. It is far more meaningful to deal with a grammar problem when it arises in the course of a writing project where the student has a vested, personal commitment. Then the skill learning is relevant and motivation improves. Learning tends to speed up, and knowledge tends to be retained longer, because the activity meets all the basic criteria of a true learning situation.

By the same token, it is important to make the real world connection as concrete as possible. This can be accomplished by involving the community in the learning environment as much as possible. Field trips are an ideal way to do this, provided of course that the trip is appropriately set up and conducted. There must be pre-trip activities to reinforce interest and to set learning goals, that is, the motivation and the context for the trip. The trip, for example, must be integral to the focus topic, and the students should know what outcomes are expected in terms of learning and behavior. The trip should be conducted so as to meet those outcomes. After the trip, there should be immediate follow up and review with respect to expected and even unexpected outcomes.

If certain financial, legal, or logistical conditions within a particular school system make field trips difficult, try bringing the community into the classroom. Every community is rich with resource people who would love to share their expertise and their experiences with students, particularly with students who have expressed a definite affinity for a topic relevant to those people's interests. In many cases, all you have to do is ask - and the act of asking, as you will see in the chapter on Adopt-a-Guest, can become a valuable learning experience for your students!

As a slight aside, involving the community directly in the school has advantages that extend beyond the students in a particular whole-learning program. A community that feels welcome in the school, indeed, that feels it is a true part of the school, will be much better prepared to support that school in myriad ways.

So, here then are the basic tenets of a whole-learning program; tenets designed to augment all five characteristics of a true learning experience:

—Student choice

—Central focus theme based on relationships rather than on specific disciplines

—Small, self-contained learning community with few time restraints

—Cooperative learning philosophy and activities

—Emphasis on student control of learning

—Performance reviews based on outcomes and student self-evaluation

—Real world, real work experiences

Before turning to some of the learning activities we use in the WATERSHED program to embody these tenets, the reader should be aware of a few important conditions that permeate all these activities. First, the whole-learning philosophy, as I have described it, encourages students to be responsible for their learning, to make choices, and to maintain control over their learning experience. To this end, the activities are designed to present students with challenges in the form of a particular outcome and with a general set of guidelines to help them achieve that outcome. In most cases, however, the students themselves must determine how they will use the guidelines and how they will present their results. Specific requirements may be kept to a minimum, but expectations of quality work at all stages of the activity are emphasized as the teachers circulate among the students to answer questions, make suggestions, and point students toward relevant resources. Students are continually encouraged to evaluate their own skills and methods, as well as their progress, as they work through the learning activity; and this ongoing self-evaluation is viewed as an integral part of the entire activity.

...expectations of quality work at all stages of the activity are emphasized...

Similarly, as you read through these activities, keep in mind that they do not occur as isolated activities, but rather as integral parts of an ongoing program. Thus they have a larger context within the framework of WATERSHED. Participating students have elected to study from as many vantage points as possible local streams and their surrounding drainage areas. While this includes looking at the more obvious physical and ecological characteristics of the streams and of the land, it also involves exploring the human interactions as they have occurred and changed over time.

To structure our exploration of local watersheds, we emphasize three interrelated phases: a *Sense of Place*, a *Sense of Time*, and a *Sense of Quality*. In the first of these we concentrate on discovering the boundaries and the physical characteristics of the watershed we have decided to explore. This includes, for example, looking at and making maps of the watershed, learning to conduct water quality analyses in the stream, examining the geology and the resultant topography of the region, and becoming familiar with the plants and animals that share the area with us.

In the *Sense of Time* phase, we take a look at the ways people have interacted with the watershed in the past. We survey the cultures that have lived in the watershed, and we analyze the various ways each interpreted its relationship to the land. The emphasis is on using the information gathered in a *Sense of Place* to help understand the changes wrought in the watershed through time.

The last phase, a *Sense of Quality*, gives the students a chance to use the knowledge and skills they have gained in the first two phases to analyze how we are using the watershed today and how we may utilize it in their future. We compare the systems that affect the quality of our life in the watershed. These systems include those that constitute our own bodies, those that make up the homes in which we live, and those larger systems of the watershed itself.

This phased framework helps provide a flexible structure within which the students direct their own learning activities and share a set of cooperative experiences. In the forthcoming chapters I have placed each learning activity in the context of these phases.

With this background in mind, let us turn now to fourteen whole-learning activities you can modify to use in your classroom. ɯ

IMPORTANT - for those not in a Watershed-type setting:

As important as these characteristics of whole-learning are, I realize that not all teachers are on two-person teams sharing 40 students. Not all teachers have the freedom and flexibility I describe in the context of whole learning. Does that mean that the activities described in this book are "out-of-reach" of teachers who are in more traditional schools, with larger numbers of students and lesser amounts of time?

Not at all. All activities described in this book are directly adaptable by teachers in most classroom situations. Depending upon the circumstance, activities could become a stand-alone unit or a part of another unit on the same topic. Feel free to adapt and adopt activities as they are appropriate to your situation, but do try to stay true to whole-learning principles. Ultimately, teachers will know best how to use these activities.

A Three-Dimensional Topographic Map

2.

Building an Understanding of Topography

*Hey, Mr. Springer, this shows the **shape** of the hills!!*

The seventh grader blurting out this personalized *Eureka!* may not have streaked through the classroom, but his excitement at that moment of discovery certainly rivaled that of Archimedes. Discovery: that's what true learning is all about. Few moments are more exciting for a student or more rewarding for a teacher.

This particular moment of discovery has been repeated with varying degrees of intensity by just about every student at some point in the process of constructing three-dimensional, scale, topographic maps of a watershed. This map activity has been a successful part of WATERSHED from the very beginning because it embodies all five characteristics of true learning, it relates to innumerable other aspects of our common study, and it leads to such moments of discovery.

The activity occurs early in our year during our Sense of Place phase. Its primary purpose is to help students explore the topography of the watershed and the physical course of the stream being studied. The required result is a three-dimensional topographic map usually in the same scale as the United States Geologic Survey's (USGS) seven and one-half minute maps; that is 2000 feet per inch or 1: 24,000. However, we have successfully enlarged maps up to three times this scale.

Discovery: that's what true learning is all about.

The process begins when we present small groups of four students with USGS maps of the region including the watershed under study. We have covered these maps in self-sticking acetate so they can be used over and over. Using markers that write on plastic, the students first locate and highlight the stream itself. This provides the common point of reference for everyone. It also allows us to discuss such terms as "headwaters," "seep," and "mouth" and to relate those terms to the stream on the map.

17

A few moments are devoted to exploring the topographic maps and looking for symbols and meanings. Sometimes we direct this discussion by asking for specific information: find the highest elevation on the map or the lowest. With some groups who seem to lack experience with such maps, we spend even more time and ask them to locate well-known landmarks and then determine directions and distances to those various familiar points of reference. For some occasions we have developed a scavenger hunt of sorts involving map symbols which the students have to locate and draw. Sometimes we ask groups to create questions for other groups to solve. Of course, the group asking the question must be prepared to determine the accuracy of the response received. Again, the optional activities to familiarize students with topographic maps are virtually limitless, and the teacher gears the extent of this background work to the needs of the particular class. At this point the purposes of activities are exploration and student discovery, and teachers do not give answers. The students share answers and verify and evaluate each other's responses based on evidence from the primary resource, the map.

The teachers do not give answers. The students share answers and verify and evaluate each other's responses based on evidence from the primary resource, the map.

Somewhere in the course of this preliminary examination of the maps, the question of contour lines inevitably arises. Once *a student* asks about those funny lines that cover the map, the door is opened to discuss their form and function. It is important that students discuss what they think these contour lines represent. The teacher can, if necessary, provide clues through questions, but should not present answers. For example, the teacher can select two areas that students are familiar with; one spot that is relatively flat, the other relatively steep. Have the student groups locate the places on their map. Then ask them to compare the contour lines and simultaneously to picture the area. Then they can draw conclusions about the contour lines. The students share their observations that contour lines are tightly packed in steep areas and widely separated in flatter areas. The class reaches consensual definitions of the role of contour lines, index contour lines, and the contour interval, as well as definitions for topography and the purpose of a topographical map.

As our student's *Eureka!* proves, though some students will be able to voice these definitions, and many will appear to understand the words involved in them, some may still not fully comprehend the concepts at this point in their learning process. Unfortunately, this is typical of many learning situations. We assume too quickly that the student understands an abstract concept simply because that student can repeat a definition of it. Too often, this is where a learning activity ends, and a class is pushed on to other concepts. Little wonder that within a very short period of time the students have lost the definition – they never truly learned it.

In this case, however, having the definition is sufficient for the moment because the learning activity does *not* stop here. This is just the beginning, and the abstract concepts involved will be made more and more concrete as the activity progresses until that moment of true discovery occurs for each student.

Armed with these new concepts, the groups are challenged to devise a way to determine the boundaries of the watershed. We review the definition of a watershed, that is, all the land that drains into a given body of water. Sometimes we suggest that the students imagine themselves as raindrops: where would they have to fall to eventually run into the stream? The more directly the teacher can tie the activity to the personal experiences of the student, the better.

Then we allow groups of students time to brainstorm and to test out their various theories. The teachers circulate among the groups and observe. Questions can be answered (though it is best to encourage the students to answer their own questions) and hints or suggestions may be given to any group experiencing undue difficulty. The teacher's primary task, however, is to observe and to make mental notes about the students' individual learning styles, contributions, and reactions to the learning experience.

The amount of time allotted to this portion of the activity varies with each class and is determined by the teachers based on student success or frustration. Our experience shows this to take anywhere from five minutes to as much as twenty minutes.

Eventually, each group arrives at some method for solving the problem. We then take a few minutes to share ideas. Students are asked to first look for something positive in each suggestion before criticizing its potential shortcomings. This, by the way, is standard practice in all discussion sessions involving shared ideas and suggestions. It sets a positive tone whereby each idea receives some affirmation, and students are encouraged to amend and refine rather than reject and criticize ideas. Nothing shuts down motivation and thinking faster than rejection.

...each idea receives some affirmation, and students are encouraged to amend and refine rather than reject and criticize ideas.

Following this discussion the groups get time to determine the boundaries of the watershed. They may use whatever method they choose: their own, one they learned from another group, or some combination gleaned from the previous discussion. Depending on the size of the watershed in question, this process can take anywhere from an hour to several hours. In WATERSHED, we usually set a due date of several days later, by which time the group has to submit its outline of the watershed boundaries marked on the acetate map.

When all versions are in hand, the class meets as a whole. The groups compare their outcomes and discuss similarities and differences. The key here is that the groups have to *justify* where they placed the limits of the watershed based on concrete data from the topographic map itself. If a group is convinced that it made a miscalculation, it simply corrects the error. Ultimately each map is compared with the master map of the watershed. Mistakes, usually few by this point, are discussed and corrected. Occasionally students have found and corrected errors in the master map!

Each group now has a common outline of the watershed, one discovered independently. The outline is their creation and most students feel very proud of their accomplishment. The students' ownership and control of the learning experience are thus maintained and motivation for the next step of the process is enhanced.

The outline is their creation and most students feel very proud of their accomplishment. The students' ownership and control of the learning experience are thus maintained and motivation for the next step of the process is enhanced.

With that next step, the real work begins. Over the years we have made these maps using both small groups and individuals. Usually the choice is based on the size of the watershed in question. When we studied the Brandywine River with its 330 square mile drainage area, we divided one large map into smaller sections which we assigned to one or two students. When we studied tiny Gulph Creek, which drains only seven square miles, each student made his or her own map. The process of making the map remains the same in either case.

The students are instructed to trace their outline of the watershed onto tracing paper. This tracing is transferred to cardboard to become the base of a three-dimensional map.

While any thickness of cardboard will do, we have found that corrugated appliance boxes work best. Though this type of cardboard causes an increased vertical exaggeration, it also provides necessary strength and stability. That vertical exaggeration, by the way, is not altogether objectionable in that it helps the students see the shape of the land more clearly – particularly in a relatively flat region such as ours where the average gradient within a watershed is generally less than fifty feet per mile. Furthermore, this type of cardboard is generally available free of charge. We visit local appliance dealers who gladly donate boxes ready for discarding. Often we simply salvage and recycle boxes from supplies delivered to our own school.

This first cardboard tracing is cut out and becomes the base of the three-dimensional map and a template to be used in the next stage of the process. I recommend that the students immediately put their names on the *underside* of this base layer. If the class is working on sections of a larger map, I also recommend that a section number, compass directions (at least northern orientation), or some other identifying characteristic be marked on the underside as well. This proves invaluable when the class assembles the jigsaw puzzle of map sections later on.

The students are then instructed to determine the total change in elevation within the watershed. This total is found by subtracting the lowest elevation where the stream ends from the highest elevation found near the headwaters. This task reinforces definitions and skills from the introductory phase of this process – a connection that is pointed out to the students to demonstrate how everything they are learning has a specific and beneficial use.

Once this total is determined, the teacher instructs the students to use their base cutout as a template to make the appropriate number of additional cardboard layers they will need to complete the map. This number is found by dividing the total elevation change by the contour interval desired. We use the fifty foot index contour interval common to many USGS maps and have the students make a cardboard layer for each of these index contour lines; so, we divide the change in elevation by fifty to determine the number of layers needed. Let's say, for example, our study stream seeps from the ground on a hillside at six hundred feet above sea level and ends by flowing into a larger river at fifty feet above sea level. We subtract fifty from six hundred, getting five hundred and fifty; and we then divide that answer by the contour interval selected. Again, we generally use a fifty foot contour interval, so five hundred and fifty divided by fifty yields eleven. The student will need eleven layers in addition to the base to make a map of this hypothetical stream. Teachers should note that some USGS maps use one hundred foot index contour intervals. These work just as well, particularly in a mountainous area, or if far less detail is desired. By the same token, for greater detail, layers can be made for every single contour line or for every other contour line. Again, the teacher has to decide ahead of time the minimum degree of detail the map should show and select the corresponding contour interval to plug into the simple equation:

$$\text{number of layers required} = \frac{\text{highest elevation - lowest elevation}}{\text{contour interval desired}}$$

21

Once the students have their supply of basic watershed shapes representing all the elevation layers required, they begin the laborious task of carefully tracing each of the predetermined contour lines from the original map. Make sure the students tape the tracing paper to the map, as any small shift can cause large-scale errors and problems later on. Successive contours, starting with the lowest levels, should be traced on the same paper as long as possible. For one thing, this saves tracing paper. Equally important, since the contour lines of a specific region tend to parallel each other in very similar patterns, using the same piece of paper helps the student find and follow the correct lines more easily. I recommend color coding these tracings to help keep them in order and to differentiate between them in areas of steep slope where the lines run close together. Color coding also becomes increasingly important at higher elevations as the basic watershed shape disappears and scattered hilltops emerge like apparently random shapes.

As before, each contour line tracing is transferred to one of the corrugated cardboard layers and then cut out. There are several ways to make this transfer. Some students like to tape the tracing paper onto the cardboard and then poke tiny holes along the colored contour line through the tracing paper and into the cardboard. When the tracing paper is removed, the student connects the dots with a pen or pencil before cutting out the layer.

While my teaching partner prefers this method, I have witnessed two potential problems with it. First, the tracing paper is often totally destroyed by the poking procedure which jeopardizes other lines and sometimes forces the student to redo some contour line tracings. An even greater problem can arise when the tracing paper is removed and the student confronts a cardboard shape covered with little holes. Sometimes the pattern is clear, but frequently it is very confusing, particularly in areas involving multiple tributaries. This confusion can lead to frequent errors.

I prefer an alternate method. The tracing paper with the colored contour lines is taped to a cardboard layer as before. However, the student simply draws over the selected contour line once again, this time pushing down firmly with a ballpoint pen. If the student works carefully, the process leaves a distinct impression on the cardboard without destroying the tracing paper. Minor tears may occur, but these can easily be taped. The resulting impression on the cardboard is much easier to pencil over in preparation for cutting. Both ways work yet require patient and careful effort.

One word of caution regarding the cutting process. Students can easily lose track of which part of the cardboard they are keeping and which part they are to discard. To avoid this problem, I recommend to my students that they shade in regions to be discarded. I also advise them to double check with me or with another student to make sure they are correct *before* they begin to cut each layer. The old carpenter's adage, "measure twice, cut once," applies to this process as well and prevents much unnecessary frustration!

Students may also become frustrated by the difficulties of cutting through the cardboard. Sharp tools are a must, so safety instructions should be discussed before any student begins to cut. Patience is also necessary. If students use bladed tools, such as carton cutters or Exacto knives, cutting boards are necessary; and the students should be told that it is easier to make several shallow cut runs through the cardboard than to try to cut all the way through in one deep slice.

...safety instructions should be discussed before any student begins to cut.

Students should also be told not to worry about the many tiny topographic details they may see on their tracings. Given the scale, the tools, and the materials involved, those tiny details will not be visible on the final map. So, students should take care to make an accurate depiction of the general topography but not worry to the point of frustration over small details.

As each successive layer is cut out, I recommend that it be immediately glued to the layer below it. This keeps pieces from getting lost, and it makes it easier to keep the layers in order. In addition, it makes the concept of topography more immediately apparent. The students see immediate step-by-step results, increasing their understanding and enhancing motivation.

Any simple, inexpensive white glue works just fine. Care should be taken to line up edges as accurately as possible. This will save trimming later. Similarly, all edges should be glued completely to prevent areas of separation and curling which make plastering difficult.

When all the layers are in place and glued securely together, the edges should be trimmed and smoothed as much as possible. Note: if you are working on sections of a large map, the sections will have to be glued together at this point. I would recommend that the class prepare a plywood base on which to assemble and mount the larger map. This will ensure that the sections stay together and will give the map the stability it will need.

For smaller maps, the cardboard base is sufficient.

The entire map is then covered in a plaster or spackling compound. This should be done in several thin layers, each of which is allowed to dry thoroughly before the next is applied. If the plaster is put on too thickly or

if a new layer is placed over a layer that has not completely dried, it may crack. I prefer a pre-mixed spackling compound because it is easy for the students to use, it cleans up with water, and it is not as heavy as plaster of paris when it dries.

As each layer of plaster is applied, it should be worked carefully into the streambed ravines so as to coat but not fill them to the point where they disappear. Ridges and fingerprints should be smoothed out. After two or three coats of plaster have been applied, the "steps" of the cardboard will disappear and the truer form of the land will take shape.

Once the plastering is complete, minor errors can be corrected using sandpaper or your cutting tools. The sides of the map can be sanded.

Now it is time to paint!

I recommend using acrylic paints. First, they are water-based, clean up easily, and do not require fume-laden solvents or turpentine. Second, they mix easily to yield a great variety of colors. Third, when dry, they form a plastic coating over the plaster which seals and protects it from chips and cracks. While I like acrylics, other forms of enamels will work just as well. The choice is up to the teacher and may well hinge on what is readily or financially available. Note, however, that the type of plaster used may have restrictions as to the types of paint it will accept.

The opportunities at this point both for individual artistic expression and for depicting alternative aspects of the watershed are virtually unlimited. For example, in WATERSHED we have the students determine underlying geological formations and color code the sides of their map to show where these rock formations are and how they affect topography. Students could just as readily paint their map in the manner of USGS maps with areas of green for woodlands, pink for urban areas, and white for open space. The students can choose the season they wish to depict and select colors accordingly.

Once the basic color scheme has been determined and painted on the map, an infinite number of details can be added depending on the class's particular goals: roads, landmarks, anything deemed important to the specific study in progress. But don't forget to put in the stream and all its tributaries! This can be accomplished effectively by using a tiny brush or a calligraphy pen with extra care taken to keep the lines of small streams as appropriately thin and delicate as possible.

Voilá ! The student now has a finished three-dimensional topographic map of his or her own making – a tangible product of which to be proud.

Upon completion of the map, students should be asked to review their work. This can be done in writing or in group or individual discussions. Regardless of the method chosen, this performance review should require students to evaluate the quality of their map itself, and the quality of their efforts throughout the process. Students should discuss which aspects of the project they found difficult, what problems they encountered, what concepts they did not understand, and specific ways to improve their performance on subsequent projects.

In WATERSHED, this anecdotal review (p. 26) is seen as a crucial part of the entire learning activity, perhaps the most crucial part in the long run. From it the student learns about performance skills and abilities that transcend the specific project and which can be applied to any of life's endeavors. As a meaningful description of the student's activities and progress, this narrative review becomes part of a student's record in place of a grade.

The map also serves from this point on as a reference resource. Students can use it continually to note locations discussed in future lessons or visited on field trips. This serves at least two purposes. First, by continually referring to their own map, students see the connections between past learning experiences and new ones. In addition, their map helps them maintain a personal connection to those experiences; and it is that personal connection to learning that promotes the ultimate internalization of knowledge that constitutes true learning. Each time students pick up their maps, they relive, at least briefly, that wonderful moment of self-discovery that brought a concept to life. ɯ

TOPOGRAPHICAL MAP ASSESSMENT

NAME: _____ Date:_____

1. Describe **your** role in this project. Be specific and tell what you actually did:

2. Describe the easiest part of this project:

3. What part seemed most difficult for you? Why was it difficult?

4. How did you overcome the difficulty?

5. What advice would you give other students who want to make a map like this?

6. What do you think you learned from this project?

7. Overall, how well do you think your map turned out?

Rock Concerts

3.

Singing the Praises of Geology

*W*ho could forget such timeless rock favorites as **Rockin' Robin** or **Rock Around the Clock**, or those wonderful television themes from **The Brady Bunch** or **The Flintstones**?

We will, we will rock you with incredible information about the very ground under your feet. With this remarkable concert series you can trace the history of rock. Learn about the cycles rock has endured through the ages. Hear how rock has shaped our land and our lives. Experience the heat and the pressures that gave birth to rock. Be moved by the sometimes shocking, always powerful forces of nature that continue to influence our world each and everyday. And if you order now, we'll throw in absolutely free your very own tour shirt and an all-expense-paid trip to the rock site of your choice …

Each year, our rock concerts prove to be one of our most popular, successful, and memorable learning activities. We present the concert series as one of the performance outcomes in the Sense of Place phase which opens our WATERSHED year. The primary purpose, clearly, is to explore the geologic underpinnings of our region and the ways various rock formations affect the area's topography and the streams we study.

The activity begins very early in the school year with the innocent request that all students find a "special" rock somewhere, sometime during their travels in the first few weeks of school. Because we spend so much time visiting local streams during September, the students have numerous opportunities to find a rock that appeals to them. Sometimes we read to the class a short children's book entitled *Everyone Needs A Rock,* by Byrd Baylor. This cute little book describes ten amusing "rules" for finding your perfect rock - rules such as: it can't be too large or too small, it has to feel lumpy in your pocket, and it has to look good by itself in the bathtub. Sometimes as a way to generate interest we simply share our own special rocks as examples, telling the story behind each rock and the memories each evokes.

Over the next few weeks the students find their special rocks and show them to us. We record the rock type to use later to form groups. We also use the rocks for several related writing exercises. For example, to practice the effective use of details, we have students write a paragraph describing their rock. We then line rocks up on a table and have students read their paragraph out loud. As each student reads, the rest of the class, or a chosen representative, tries to identify the reader's rock from the line-up based only on details given in the descriptive paragraph.

Similarly, we have students draw their rocks as a way to reinforce observation skills and to practice sketching techniques. Such multiple activities tie the experience together and reestablish the inherent links among skills from the artificially separated subject areas.

Once everyone has a special rock, we use these selections to form the rock groups. Students who selected a form of Quartzite, for example, are grouped together. We usually end up with six to eight groups that correspond to the major rock formations in our region.

At this point the class receives the instructions for their rock concerts. The group must research their rock formation and gather as much information about it as they can. The information must include its age, how it formed, its mineral contents, its hardness, and other physical characteristics, where it is found, how it affects topography, and how it is used by people.

All this research will be presented to the class in the form of a "concert" appearance. During this concert, students perform an original rock lyric to the tune of a popular song. The lyric contains much of the pertinent information. After the performance of the song, the group reviews the information in a somewhat more straightforward manner so the class can take notes. This presentation must include a geological timeline showing the history of the rock relative to other world occurrences or conditions, a sample of the rock, a poster or other visual aide displaying the important information, and a tour shirt showing where the rock formation can be found in our region.

To prepare for this concert, students first have time to organize themselves within their group. This is one of their first opportunities to work on the organizational and cooperative group skills they will use all year, so we spend some time circulating among the groups to advise them as they discuss ways to work together achieve their goals. It is important to help students with cooperative concepts. We discuss the notion of compromise, for example, and positive ways to listen and react to suggestions. We talk with groups about divisions of labor and delegation of responsibilities, as well as about the role and responsibilities of leaders. The students wrestle with complex issues such as how to get a less than enthusiastic or an uncooperative student to participate, or how to ensure that everyone does his or her fair share of the work.

It is important to help students with cooperative concepts. We discuss the notion of compromise, for example, and positive ways to listen and react to peoples' suggestions.

It is very important to note that we do not preach at this point. Rather, we encourage the students to invent strategies that work for them. We can certainly ask questions and make suggestions, but the learning must be theirs, including the opportunity to make mistakes.

Obviously a sufficient amount of time must be allotted for research. We are fortunate to have a fairly extensive collection of textual and electronic resources in our classroom that students are free to use. We also have access to the school library and the community library, and we encourage small groups of students to use these resources as well. The amount of time allowed for organization, for research, and for preparation of the concert, of course, must be gauged by the teacher. There is no magic formula. Not being restricted by forty minute class periods allows us a great deal of flexibility, and we usually provide three to four weeks for the entire process to unfold. In a more typical classroom this process could take anywhere from three to five weeks, depending on how much of each class period is devoted to the groups' activities.

In addition to classroom or library research, each group takes a half-day field trip to visit local areas where its rock formation is found. This gives them a chance to collect rock samples and to see for themselves how their rock influences the topography, the vegetation, and sometimes the use of the land. Besides the learning that occurs with respect to group dynamics, this first-hand experience is the most important aspect of the learning activity. Given the overall context, this short field experience is the aspect that most clearly embodies the fundamentals of the *whole-learning* philosophy at its finest.

The students have a wonderful time selecting their song and writing the new lyrics. They work out and jealously guard the secrets of their performance routines. They design and make their tour T-shirts using markers, fabric paints, sequins, and even dyes.

29

Geological timelines of all sorts begin to appear throughout the room ranging in appearance from more traditional charts to circular clock-like posters to three-dimensional "towers of time."

Rock samples are displayed, and posters receive their finishing touches.

Concert days are truly an experience. Each group is allotted whatever time it needs to perform its song and present its information. Usually the songs are backed by taped music, but on occasion we have had student guitarists, keyboardists, and even flutists provide the musical accompaniment. Taped or live, these concerts are as entertaining as they are informative. We videotape the concerts and show some of them to parents at the next open house. We also use these videos as a way to help groups assess their own presentations.

After each song, the class takes notes as the group formally reviews the important facts about its rock formation. Some groups employ a traditional report format for this phase of the project; some creative groups have developed presentations involving interviews with the rock musicians, for example, or mock newscasts. There is no limit to the creativity students can display when given the freedom and the time to express themselves.

There is also no limit to the pride of accomplishment and the sense of ownership the students display upon completion of this activity. Though they do the normal self-evaluation, the truest proof of their successful learning is witnessed throughout the year. For the remainder of the year and beyond, whenever we mention a particular rock or a place where that rock is found, the students react immediately with mini-choruses of their song or some other reference to the fact that it is *their* rock. And isn't that what true learning is all about?

After all, who could ever forget such rock classics? ⨆

Water Fair

Sharing the Fun of Learning

4.

A s discussed earlier, the very heart of the whole-learning philosophy is having students cooperate to create tangible products illustrating what they have discovered and learned through their first-hand experiences and then, in turn, teach others. A true whole-learning program establishes an interrelated series of such projects that build on each other for both skill and concept development. Thus far, I have described two such interlocking projects. The first of these, the three-dimensional topographical map project, required a cooperative effort to create a particularly tangible and specific product. In the case of large watersheds such as the Brandywine, the product was a single class map. With smaller watersheds students create individual, but identical maps. Whether it is a single map or many personal maps, the product is evaluated on its accuracy and the process of working together.

In the second learning activity I discussed how small groups of students cooperate to present information in a series of similar rock concerts. This is one step above the map project in terms of the cooperative efforts required, and also in terms of the product itself. On one hand, accuracy still counts. Students must present correct, calculated information about the rock formations. Furthermore, the information contained in these concerts must correlate directly to their mapping experiences. Not surprisingly, most groups do incorporate one of their three-dimensional maps into their presentation. However, beyond this level of content accuracy, groups must now achieve a level of creativity in their presentation that was not present in the mapping project. Each group's rock concert, while similar in terms of the type of information presented, is quite different.

For the third major learning activity in our Sense of Place phase of WATERSHED, we move to yet a higher plane of process and product. The Water Fair is a class effort that requires small groups to cooperate in creating the final product. That final product is a daylong, student-produced exposition centered on the characteristics and importance of water.

We begin the activity as a full class in one of several ways. For example, sometimes we simply begin by brainstorming about the ways we use water and then turn these ideas into a discussion of water's importance. From the more obvious notion of its significance to our lives, we turn next to its characteristics. What do we really know about water, this most precious of elements? As a class, we usually discover quickly just how little we really know! Once students realize that, it is easy to throw down the gauntlet and challenge them to learn more. At this point we introduce the idea of the Water Fair as an enjoyable way to share what we learn.

As an alternative introductory activity, I like to start with a little game we call "Facts in Five." The only drawback to this activity is the need for readily available resources. We are fortunate to have extensive resource materials in our classroom. If you do not have this luxury, perhaps you could arrange to use your school library. To start this game, each student receives a blank 3X5 card. Students put their names on these cards. Then they are given five minutes to search available resources to find at least one *new* fact about water. They must record this fact, along with its source (magazine, book, article) on cards.

It is important to emphasize several points here before setting students loose. First, the facts should be ones students did not already know. While there is no way to verify this, most students will comply either because they are sincerely interested, or because they do not want to appear stupid in front of their peers by presenting a fact that everyone already knows. A second point of emphasis: if time allows, students might want to find more than one new fact, just in case someone else finds and shares the same fact first. Third, it is crucial that students record the source of the information. This enables the class to verify for accuracy any surprising, questionable, or conflicting information. In addition, it introduces and reinforces the research skills of documenting sources in footnotes and producing a bibliography. If these skills have already been taught, you can require the students to use either the proper footnote or bibliographical form. Indeed, you can use this activity to teach those forms even as you are introducing Water Fair.

Once the instructions are given and any questions answered, students are allowed five minutes to find their facts. Obviously, the teacher can allow whatever time is appropriate. If you are in your school library, this activity could serve as an orientation to that facility; in the library you might want to provide a longer period for the students to explore available resources. We use five minutes because it is quick and easy, and we are right in our own classroom using materials familiar to the students.

When the allotted time has elapsed, the class reconvenes to share facts, having student volunteers list each new one on the board. Throughout the discussion we ask students to tell us where they found their facts as well. This helps all of us learn about materials we might not have discovered and validates the request that students record their sources.

Once all the facts are listed, we allow students a few moments to work together to look for relationships, categories, or ways to group the water facts together. We then discuss their suggested groupings and help the class reach a consensus. From these categories groups are created. Each group must then devise an activity to illustrate and demonstrate facts in its category. This activity will become a booth at our Water Fair.

Tangentially, we usually collect all the "Facts in Five" cards and have a student volunteer make a poster to display them in the room. The individual work of each student becomes part of a class learning resource reinforcing factual content as well as the importance of our cooperative efforts.

The groups spend time over the next several weeks researching their area and designing both their activity and their booth for the Water Fair. Early in this process, and at intervals along the way we gather representatives from each group and have them share their ideas with each other. This allows groups to see if there is any unnecessary overlap of content or format. If groups have similar ideas for their respective activities, as sometimes happens, they have to work out ways to compromise to ensure that each booth's experience will be unique, as well as informative and enjoyable. In addition, each group designs an invitation asking the other teams in the school to schedule a time to visit our Water Fair.

Over the years students have designed many kinds of booths covering many different water concepts. For instance, one group had a taste testing activity using different types of bottled water and tap water. Groups have set up experiments to demonstrate heating and cooling capacities of water. Others have asked students to weigh different volumes of water and then graph the results to reach a class determination of the density of water.

We have had games showing how water erodes different soils, and ones showing how different materials react with water.

Throughout the discussion we ask students to tell us where they found their facts as well. This helps all of us learn about materials we might not have discovered and validates the request that students record their sources.

One of my all-time favorites was the group who built a giant bubble-making apparatus out of inexpensive PVC piping and used it to demonstrate the concept of surface tension. We had a wonderful time creating huge soap bubbles! There is no end to the possibilities here, nor to the creativity students display as they turn hard research into enjoyable activities.

A few days before the scheduled Water Fair we have a dress rehearsal. Each group sets up its booth and presents its demonstration for the rest of us. We require each student to keep a personal record of his or her reactions to each booth. The students must also write down the important information about water presented by each booth and activity.

We collectively critique each group's presentation and offer suggestions for improvements. The groups then have a few days to make adjustments before the day of the fair arrives.

On the day of the Water Fair, the groups set up their respective booths around the room. We often have booths outside, too, but that may or may not be a possibility for other teachers.

As mentioned already, we always invite other classes or grade levels to visit our Water Fair, and almost every year we have had several classes accept the invitation.

This adds even more significance to the event as students now face a wider audience. It also provides our students with the chance to present their work several times during the day. This allows them to rotate responsibilities, hone their presentation, and further internalize their information.

At the end of the day, time is allotted first for clean-up and for wrap-up. In the summary session, groups should first meet on their own to evaluate themselves. From their own point of view, how well was their booth received and how well do they think it conveyed the important water concepts?

Then, as individuals, everyone in the class should have the opportunity to praise and critique all the booths. We do this using a form that lists the booths and asks the students to describe something they liked about each and something they think could be improved about each. After students have had the chance to record their own thoughts, we have a class discussion of the whole Water Fair process. The goal, as always, is to point out strategies that worked particularly well and to make positive suggestions to improve aspects of the project that did not succeed as well. We also use this discussion as an opportunity to preview coming attractions – other similar class learning activities such as the Lenape Feast Day or the American Origins projects.

Finally, this same wrap-up discussion lets us review one last time the facts we have learned and shared about the nature and the importance of water. Content and process truly merge. What is more, the students have maintained control over every phase of the experience making a memorable and enjoyable learning activity for us all and setting the stage for future group activities. ⱳ

Lenape Feast Day 5.
A Celebration of Native American Culture

*M*r. Springer, are you **sure** this will work?
We've been working this bow thing for a long …
Wait.… I think we've got it! — Yes!!

A thin wisp of smoke, a glowing ember, a gentle breath, and the dried fibers burst into flame.

Moments later the class encircles our ceremonial fire, now blazing within its pit next to the softball field, and we listen with excited solemnity as a group of nine students recite a native American greeting to the day. One by one, these nine students welcome the sun, the moon, the sky, the water, the land, the plants, the animals, the fire, and finally all of us to our Lenape Feast Day. The Lenape, who inhabited this region long before the Europeans arrived, held such feast days each autumn to celebrate the bounty of their harvest.

Like those Lenape, we, too, celebrate a harvest of sorts. This day in late November or early December is the culmination of a month's worth of research and preparation. As you will see, a great deal of labor and creativity goes into this learning activity, and many benefits accrue from it as well. It is truly a celebration.

Preparations for Feast Day began in late October, even as we continued our work on the Rock Concerts and the Water Fair activities in the Sense of Place phase of our WATERSHED year. In fact, the structure for the Feast Day activity is very similar to that of the Water Fair, so the transition is very easily accomplished and the procedures complement and reinforce each other.

The class is introduced to the project through a general description of previous years' projects. We explain that groups need to be formed to re-

search and then present information about particular aspects of Lenape life. Students brainstorm possible topics for these groups and then determine the actual ones they want to pursue. For example, we usually end up having a group assigned to food. This same group assumes responsibility for describing the Lenape diet, including the types of food they consumed, how they obtained the food, and how they prepared it. Another group may take on the task of storytelling, which often accompanied meals in Lenape culture. Another group might be made responsible for Lenape clothing or crafts, yet another for Lenape games, and another for learning how Lenape built their fires or their shelters. The number of groups is up to the teacher and the class to determine together based on class size and on the number of students required to handle the topic. We tend to limit ourselves to four, five, or six groups.

Once formed, the groups assume all responsibility for researching their topic and for devising appropriate ways to share it with the rest of us...

At any rate, students then volunteer for the different groups based on their own interests. Once formed, the groups assume all responsibility for researching their topic and for devising appropriate ways to share it with the rest of us on Feast Day. We start this research process by asking each group to write questions about its topic.

We also ask the groups to list questions about the other topics as well, and we share these latter issues so groups know what other people want to learn about their topic. We record all these questions on posters and display them in the room for everyone to see. This helps keep our respective groups' goals in front of them, but it also helps people share information if they find something that relates to another group's topic.

As with the Water Fair, a smaller committee of a representative from each of the groups meets periodically to plan the day itself and to coordinate the activities of the groups.

In addition to their group responsibilities. each student is required to produce a Lenape artifact based on individual research. These artifacts, each accompanied by a 6x8 card describing the object and its significance, become our Lenape Museum which we tour as part of the Feast Day activities. Over the years we have had artifacts such as pots and bowls made from local stream clay, corn husk dolls, snowshoes made of sticks and leather thongs, stone tools and weapons, gourd rattles, shell eating utensils, model wigwams, articles of clothing, moccasins, carved models of dugout canoes, leather totem pouches, shell and bead forms of wampum – the list goes on and on. The main point is that these artifacts be as authentic as possible, and that they be made by students.

Every student is also asked to choose a Lenape name. We are fortunate to have discovered some fairly extensive vocabulary lists and a tape of spoken Lenape. From these each student selects a name and draws an appropriate identifying pictograph. We display these pictographs throughout the room beginning early in the process so we can learn each other's Lenape name by Feast Day. This helps personalize the activity for each student.

To aid the students in their research, we again make use of local resources. Some years we have guest speakers visit the classroom to work with the various groups. Some years we visit one of two nearby nature centers that offers programs about the Lenape lifestyle for school groups. In addition to these firsthand experiences, we read various sources together as a class, and the students visit the school library to research their respective topics. At the same time, students also begin to make their artifact and to work on their first American Diary entry, a day in the life of a young Lenape in the early seventeenth century (see Chapter 7).

By the time Feast Day arrives, all the groups have prepared ways to demonstrate their knowledge to the rest of us. The organizing committee has set up a schedule based on the needs of the various groups. This schedule allows every student the chance to present some aspect of his or her own group's activity and have time to experience all the other groups' presentations as well. As with the Water Fair, we send out invitations to the other teams in the school and to parents and administrators as well. One year, by coincidence, we even had a group of visiting teachers and students from Ohio join us on Feast Day.

The day usually begins with the lighting of the fire, as described briefly at the opening of this chapter. We secure the principal's permission, then the students dig a shallow circular pit in the sand and gravel area of the coach's box along the third base line of the softball field. We use this area for several obvious reasons. For one thing, it is open and sufficiently far away from the building and from any trees or bushes. It is sandy gravel, so no grass can catch fire or be damaged. When we are finished and the fire is extinguished, we can fill in the gravel hole, and no one can tell a fire had been there.

Once the fire is going, we gather around it for the ceremonial welcome – a paraphrased and somewhat modernized version of an original native American ritual.

After this greeting, the groups begin their respective presentations in the order determined by the organizing committee. Usually the cooking group gets the day rolling by describing Lenape foods and showing the class how that food is prepared over the fire. They use authentic recipes for common foods such as pine needle tea (sipped from large clam or mussel shells) and corn cakes baked on hot rocks near the fire.

While we eat, members of another group tell Lenape legends, just as traveling storytellers would have done four hundred years ago around a Lenape campfire. They may also teach us a Lenape song.

Lenape games were intended to teach young people the real life skills they would need to survive while providing entertainment as well.

Usually we break into groups after the food and stories. Some people go to one area of our field and learn to play various Lenape games. These games were intended to teach young people the real life skills they would need to survive while providing entertainment as well. (Whole-learning at its best!) There the students learn to thrown corncob darts through swinging grapevine wreaths. They learn to sneak up on a blindfolded "keeper of the fire." They sharpen their senses in skill games such as "Rattler" in which blindfolded players must catch the rattler by listening for the rattler's periodic movements. They challenge their reflexes and their bravery in a game called "Flinch," a game in which a small bag of pebbles is thrown gently from a leader to any one of the players circled around that leader. The players must stand with their arms folded across their chests until the bag is thrown in their direction. The leader can fake a throw, however; and if the player flinches, that is, unfolds his or her arms in premature anticipation of a toss, that player is out of the game. We have also enjoyed indoor games such as a form of "pick-up sticks" and variations on bean bag tossing games. Every year is a bit different, but the learning is the same.

While these games continue in one area, another area is devoted to the crafts group. Here students teach each other various Lenape crafts. Once again, the choice is up to the group in charge, and every year is different. One year the students did face painting and made jewelry out of natural items such as beans and shells. Another year students all made corn husk dolls from old cornstalks donated by a local farmer. Still another year we all made small leather pouches.

Meanwhile, back at the fire, that group is teaching others how to start a fire using both the bow method and the flint method. This group describes the important role fire played in Lenape life.

Another group describes the Lenape shelters, most notably the bark wigwam and smaller wickiup, and the seasonal migratory patterns that the Lenape followed. They teach the others in the class how to lash branches together. Twice groups have built a life-sized wigwam using branches and bark they collected. Another year, the students constructed their wigwam out of cardboard strips with brown paper for the "bark" covering.

A round-robin schedule usually works well for these demonstrations. This enables each student to see all the other groups and also participate in presenting his or her own group's activity.

When all the demonstrations have been enjoyed by all, we move into our museum. Generally one or two student volunteers have taken on the task of setting up this museum in the classroom, often displaying artifacts on all the available desk and table surfaces. These students also create a museum brochure that lists all artifacts and their creators. Every visitor, student, parent, or faculty member gets a copy of this attractive brochure.

Usually we all sit on the floor and let each student show his or her artifact and tell us about it. The students ask questions and compare artifacts. We take pictures of these presentations so each child can have a visual record as a momento of the Feast Day.

We take photos and videos throughout all activities of this sort. These photographs are displayed in the room for future reference and so visitors can share the experience long after it has ended. Some photos go home with our weekly comment sheets to be displayed on refrigerators or to be sent to distant relatives. We show the videos at our frequent open house evenings so working parents who were not able to attend the activity can still share in the experience. Finally, we use the videos as a learning tool by having the students view their own presentations with an eye to improving in the future.

And that brings us to the last and most important part of the entire learning activity, students' self-evaluation. In addition to evaluating their personal performances on the videos, students discuss each of the major presentation groups. We point out aspects that worked particularly well, and we make suggestions for improving facets that did not go well. Each student then writes a personal evaluation of his or her own effort and performance on the entire Feast Day project.

The effects of the activity last long after Feast Day itself is over because the major components of a true learning experience have been main-

The effects of the activity last long after Feast Day itself is over because the major components of a true learning experience have been maintained.

tained. Of course, artifacts and photos remain on display in the room for the rest of the school year; but more important, the students remember this experience with incredible vividness because they have had control over and vested interest in the entire process. They talk about it for days, weeks, and months to come. Because the learning was pleasurable at every step of the process, many continue to recall it fondly when they return to visit us years later. Attached to those vivid memories are many of the important facts and concepts we wanted them to internalize about the Lenape people who lived here long before. Like their Lenape predecessors, the students have clearly learned important life skills along the way as well: attention to nature through the dramatic changes of seasons; the importance of rituals and celebrations in defining one's culture; and the dignity that comes from doing daily, life-sustaining tasks well. ɯ

Create-A-Colony

6.

Re-Living an Area's History

That's a good spot. It will give us flat land for our corn fields, but isn't it a bit too far from the stream?

In twenty-five words or less, the student uttering these words has demonstrated an awareness of a number of remarkable concepts. Among other points, the student has recognized a relationship between the topography of an area and its potential use, in this case for agriculture. The student has further recognized a particular type of agriculture as suitable for the region, as well as an awareness of the space needed to grow that particular crop. Additionally, the student is clearly aware of a perceived need to be near water for drinking, irrigation, or for some other use such as power or transportation. Finally, the student has shown the ability to use all these informational concepts as analytical criteria for evaluating a specific location. All of this in fewer than twenty-five words! This demonstrates the powerful learning potential involved in one of my all-time favorite WATERSHED whole-learning activities, Create-A-Colony.

To place this project into context, it is the second major group project in the Sense of Time phase of our year. Students have spent the first third of the year developing a Sense of Place: an understanding of the topographical and geophysical characteristics of our region. They have also examined, through the Lenape Feast Day described in the previous chapter, the first human inhabitants of our area and their relationship with the land. Now we turn to the arrival of Europeans to this region and the beginnings of those settlements that ultimately led to the creation of our country as we know it.

In our particular area of Pennsylvania, the first permanent European settlements were established by the Swedes, so I will describe the project in that context. Teachers will note, of course, that the project will work equally well in whatever region and with whatever colonizing group exists in your area.

We begin the project with a bit of play acting - a little living history, if you will. We call the class together and distribute to them a letter we have hypothetically received from Queen Christina, the twelve-year-old monarch who controlled Sweden in the 1630s. This letter, which I read aloud as the class follows along, constitutes a royal decree to establish a colony for Sweden in the New World. In addition to basic background information, the letter explains the purposes of the colony and certain conditions which must be met. In essence, it establishes the general guidelines of the project and the expected performance outcomes.

January 1, 1637   *Stockholm, Sverige*

By decree of Her Royal Highness, Queen Christina, Monarch of all Sverige, and of Her Regent, His Lordship Axel Oxensteirna, you are hereby ordered to commence preparations for the timely establishment of a trading colony in the New World. Her Majesty graciously extends to you the use of two ships, the Kalmar Nyckel and the Fogel Grip, for said purpose; and She commands you forthwith to outfit these ships according to your needs and to select and provision a crew of thirty-six able-bodied men to accompany you on this most important venture.

It is Her Majesty's wish that the colony be established by the spring of 1638 in that region of the New World at or near the 40th degree of latitude, a safe distance south of the Dutch settlements of New Amsterdam and north of the English settlements of Virginia. It is Her Majesty's further wish that peaceful trading with the native population, as well as the thorough search for animal, vegetable and mineral resources begin with all due expediency; that our sovereign nation might continue to prosper and to compete successfully with those other European nations currently benefiting from the riches of the New World.

Thus, by Royal decree, you have until [insert appropriate date] of this year to submit for Her Royal Majesty's approval a crew register of both names and occupations; as well as a full and complete reckoning of all such provisions as you wish to secure which will, in your opinion, ensure the success of the colony in the wilderness you will find and in the face of possible enemies who may greet you, both native and European. This listing must include specific and separate accounts for food, clothing, shelter, tools, weapons and barter items.

In addition, you will be expected to submit a full and detailed account at a later date of your voyage to the Americas and, by the end of the first year, an account of all that you have found and accomplished. Further instructions on these reports will follow closer to the time of your departure.

Her Majesty expresses Her complete confidence in you and your abilities to fulfill the requirements of this critical endeavor; and to that end here affixes Her Royal seal that all may aid you as you may require.

As you can see, the letter establishes the basic requirements of the project framed by historically accurate details and tone. In addition to this letter, the students receive a copy of the following instructions phrased in more recognizable words and a more accessible style to ensure that students clearly understand the outcomes expected.

CREATE-A-COLONY SPECIFIC INSTRUCTIONS

Your group will make plans to create a colony in your watershed area. The purposes of the colony are to set up trade with the Lenape, to search for minerals, to grow tobacco and food, to raise sheep, and to keep an eye on the Dutch colonies in New Amsterdam. You must accomplish specific preliminary tasks in the following order:

1. Decide what types of crafts, trades, and occupations would be most necessary to the survival of a small community isolated in the wilderness.
2. Decide how many people of each trade (from #1) you wish to take with you. Keep in mind that your total colony may not exceed 36 people. Make up appropriate Swedish names for all of your colonists. [In preparation for later parts of this project, you should select one of these colonists as your own personal character.]
3. Decide what tools, weapons, clothing, food and other equipment or provisions you will need to take with you. You will not be resupplied for at least a year. You have only two small ships to carry your settlers and their supplies, so you must choose carefully. Also list types of food and materials you hope or expect to find in the New World. Remember also, this is 1637, not the present day: supplies must be ones that were in fact available then!
4. These lists must be turned in to us by _____.
5. Once these lists are in and approved, you will receive your instructions for sailing and settling.

Equipped with these instructions, students form into groups of four to six. Usually we allow students to select their own groups for this project, but sometimes extenuating circumstances have necessitated a bit of creative engineering. This aspect of the project is up to the teacher's discretion based on the needs of and expectations for the particular class. Clearly we favor student selection to allow a sense of control.

Once groups are formed, students begin the process of discussing and creating the various required lists. The teacher circulates among groups and may make suggestions or answer questions that arise. Most important, the teacher should play devil's advocate and *ask* questions – questions that encourage students to consider aspects of the situation they may have overlooked. Ultimately, however, the decisions must be theirs.

The teacher should also be prepared to direct students to appropriate resources. I have a book of Swedish names, for example, that students use to create their many characters. When we are asked, we provide information about the actual size of the two ships. We are fortunate to possess a naval architect's drawing of the *Kalmar Nyckel*, for example, presenting the basic dimensions of the ship. With the math teacher's help, students figure out how much cargo space they can fill. We frequently send students off to the library, at their request, to find out information about types and sizes of barrels, for instance, or to research what life was like in Sweden in the seventeenth century – this latter assignment to help them determine what types of food, clothing, and supplies the actual settlers would have brought.

To augment all this research, we take several field trips. We visit the site of the first settlement, located not too far from us in modern day Wilmington, Delaware. We visit a shipyard where a replica of the *Kalmar Nyckel* is being constructed, and we take a trip to the American-Swedish Historical Museum in Philadelphia to hear more about the original colonists and to view artifacts from that colony. These field trips add realism to the students' work and show them a connection between their study and real world activities. I encourage teachers to use structured, topic-significant field trips whenever possible to increase motivation, to enhance the overall enjoyment of the activity, and to establish real world connections.

In addition to these trips, we spend time as a class reading together and discussing numerous resources that describe Sweden's colonial efforts. We examine as well some resources that provide a general background to the overall period of European colonial expansion into America. These resources include maps, paintings, videos, movies, diaries, and books, and guest speakers. In short, we try to make available to the students as much information as possible for them to use as they create a hypothetical colony. But the majority of the time is given to the groups to discuss this information. They have to work together, analyze data and conditions, and make decisions to ensure the group's success. This means that they have to decide what determines "success" and what factors could jeopardize or enhance their chances of achieving it.

Once these decisions are made and the required lists are in, the class gets together to discuss what each group has accomplished. Groups learn from each other as they see and hear aspects they may have missed. Last minute changes are made and the lists are ultimately approved.

Students are then required to write the first of two American Diaries relating to this project. For a more complete explanation of these diaries, see Chapter 7. For now, suffice to say that each student assumes the personality of one of the colonists. Again, it is important to allow the student to choose the character he or she wants. The student then writes a journal entry or a letter "home" to Sweden describing the voyage over to America. In preparation, students have read several actual diary accounts of similar voyages, they have seen pictures and models of the ships, they have traced the sea route on the world map, and they have read historians' descriptions of the voyage.

While on the surface this would appear to be an individual activity – and it is to the extent that each student writes his or her own paper – it is also a continuation of the group project, because the papers of a given group must concur on details. Each student can select the date of his or her letter or journal entry, but that date must be within the historically accurate period, and it must reflect the character's knowledge of his particular group's experiences to that point. If, for example, one student in a group writes that a certain character died of sickness early in the voyage, another student cannot have that character appear at a later date. If a student says the weather was stormy in February, the rest of the group's papers must agree. So, the group must work together to coordinate all basic information. In a sense, this part of the project reflects real life situations in that the individual retains a great deal of freedom and control but simultaneously has a responsibility to enhance the group's efforts as well.

In a sense, this part of the project reflects real life situations in that the individual retains a great deal of freedom and control but simultaneously has a responsibility to enhance the group's efforts as well.

In addition to reinforcing the content of this project, the American Diaries entries provide an opportunity for the students to practice numerous writing skills. Over and above the obvious ones of spelling, grammar, and mechanics, this type of narrative writing requires skills of plot and character development. Dialogue is frequently involved, and descriptive techniques are of paramount importance. In addition, the writing is seen as an integral portion of the overall project. It is not an isolated assignment, but one which advances the group's efforts while helping the individual student as well. This makes writing more enjoyable and more meaningful to the student; and that, in turn, leads to higher motivation, a greater willingness to write and rewrite, and ultimately to improved writing skills.

As individuals are writing their personal accounts of the voyage, the group continues on to the second stage of the larger project. Members have to select a real place to build their colony. This site must enable them to fulfill the Queen's instructions, and the group will be called upon to justify its selection. Hence the discussion excerpt that opened this chapter. The students have to use everything they learned about the region during our Sense of Place phase and apply it to this historically realistic problem.

Having selected an appropriate site, the group then designs its colony. The class is reminded that each group will be required to present to the New Sweden Trading Company Board of Directors an "account" of its first year's accomplishments. Keeping in mind that these directors (played by the rest of the class and the teachers) have never been to the New World, no knowledge can be taken for granted. Furthermore, since these directors have invested great sums of money to back this colonial trading venture, they will want a full and complete description of all aspects of life in the New Sweden colony. The group must be certain to account for its accomplishments with respect to the Queen's instructions; most notably the success in trading with the Lenape, the search for valuable natural resources, and relations with the Dutch. This report must include drawings or models of the fort and other buildings, and maps of the region to show where their fort and fields are located relative to Lenape villages or trading paths, natural resources, and Dutch settlements. Beyond these visual aides, the group is encouraged to make or draw any artifacts, maps, pictures, or charts that will make the report more interesting and informative – in short, to show off as much as possible of life in this region three hundred and fifty years ago. The idea is to merge requirements with freedom of choice and expression to increase the students' sense of control and vested interest in the learning activity.

AMERICAN DIARY

#1

THE VOYAGE

Name:_____

Purpose: *Special Attention Areas:*

_____   Imaginative / Narrative   Mechanical:_____
_____   Sensory / Descriptive
_____   Practical / Informative   Organizational:_____
_____   Analytical / Expository
                                          Stylistic:_____

Audience: Content:_____

         General:_____

         Specific:_____   Date Due:_____

Assignment: Using information you have learned from our reading, our discussions and our trips, describe as fully and as clearly as you can the life of a Swedish colonist during his first year in New Sweden (1638 - 1639). Use sensory images and specific details to make the time and the colony seem real to your readers. Don't forget to mention the voyage, and make sure your descriptions and facts agree with those of everyone else in your Create-A-Colony group.

BE THERE !!

The paper should be no longer than two typed, double-spaced pages, and it **must be typed**. [Use your resources at home or the computers here, but plan ahead!]

Remember, this paper represents the second in a series of short descriptive writings you will eventually use to create one longer work of historical fiction near the conclusion of our Sense of Time. The more information and detail you work into these short papers now, the easier it will be to construct the longer paper later.

Use this sheet for your preliminary notes and rough copy; attach any extra sheets as needed. Finally, when you are ready to submit your edited draft, attach it at the back, behind this sheet and any other preliminary sheets.

AMERICAN DIARY

#2

NEW SWEDEN

Name:_____

Purpose:

_____ Imaginative / Narrative
_____ Sensory / Descriptive
_____ Practical / Informative
_____ Analytical / Expository

Special Attention Areas:

Mechanical:_____

Organizational:_____

Stylistic:_____

Content:_____

Audience:

General:_____
Specific:_____

Date Due:_____

Assignment: Using information you have learned from our reading, our discussions and our trips, describe as fully and as clearly as you can the life of a Swedish colonist during his first year in New Sweden (1638 - 1639). Use sensory images and specific details to make the time and the colony seem real to your readers. Don't forget to make sure your descriptions and facts agree with those of everyone else in your Create-A-Colony group.

BE THERE !!

The paper should be no longer than two typed, double-spaced pages, and it **must be typed.** [Use your resources at home or the computers here, but plan ahead!]

Remember, this paper represents the third in a series of short descriptive writings you will eventually use to create one longer work of historical fiction near the conclusion of our Sense of Time. The more information and detail you work into these short papers now, the easier it will be to construct the longer paper later.

Use this sheet for your preliminary notes and rough copy; attach any extra sheets as needed. Finally, when you are ready to submit your edited draft, attach it at the back, behind this sheet and any other preliminary sheets.

Just before these reports are presented, students write their second American Diary with respect to these early colonists. This diary is a letter home to Sweden describing the colonists' first year in America. The student uses the same character developed in the previous American Diary. Students have a great deal of freedom concerning what aspects of life they elect to describe, but each individual account must agree with the group's upcoming, overall presentation and with each of the other individual accounts from that group. Required at this point in the project, the diary serves as another opportunity for each student to review the group's decisions and helps each student prepare for the final group presentation.

These final presentations are always a sight to behold! The students go all out to make their presentations as realistic as possible, often going so far as to arrive in costumes in the roles of the Swedish colonists they represent. Some groups bring in authentic food, and most groups relate clever stories about their colonists' adventures with the Lenape or the Dutch. In addition, each group shows off its maps, drawings, charts, and models as tangible evidence of its comprehension and effort.

These presentations give all students a chance to practice public speaking skills, as everyone is required to make a significant oral contribution. Sometimes we videotape these presentations and have students evaluate themselves later. The presentations also allow us all to see what everyone has accomplished, and each presentation reinforces information we have studied.

The presentations frequently initiate lively debates, too. Groups may be called upon to defend their choice of a site or perhaps the way they designed their fort. This leads groups to evaluate their own decisions as compared to those of the other groups. By so doing, the students realize alternatives, particularly procedural ones, they can adopt or adapt in future efforts.

Once all the presentations have been given, we turn to that all important evaluation phase. Actually, as we have seen, the evaluation is ongoing from the start of the activity. Nevertheless, this more formal evaluation requires the students to look back over the entire project. They review those aspects that gave them difficulty and try to determine why those areas were difficult. They note those parts of the project they found easy to do, and they discuss things they might have done, or next time do, differently. They evaluate the cooperative process, itself: what sorts of problems did the *group* encounter, how did they try to overcome those problems, were they successful, what other means might they have tried. These are issues they address to bring personal meaning to the entire learning experience.

This project leads directly into research activities involving the subsequent historical development of our region, some of which is described in other chapters of this book. But even when seen apart from its larger context, this project embodies all the characteristics of a true learning experience. Each year we witness progress for each student in content and skills mastery. Even more importantly, we see tremendous growth in the learning process itself for every student involved. **ɯ**

GROUP PROJECT ASSESSMENT SHEET

PROJECT: _____   DUE DATE: _____

STUDENTS: _____   _____

_____   _____

_____   _____

NOTES and IMPRESSIONS

COMPONENTS: (list)
Complete:
Neat:
Effective:

ORAL PRESENTATION:
Volume:
Organization:
Completeness:
Participation:
Originality/Creativity:
Overall Effectiveness:
Other Points:

RECOMMENDATIONS:

Hanging Timelines

Making Historical Events Tangible

7.

Surveying lengthy time spans has always presented problems. While the information is essential for a general understanding of an era or as background for another learning activity, keeping students' interest and motivation levels up is difficult in the face of an apparently endless and usually shallow stream of names, events, and dates.

Once again, whole-learning techniques can ease this dilemma. The key, as emphasized throughout this book, is to make the information significant and to give students a sense of ownership and control over it. One way to do this is to involve the students directly in the survey process; that is, have them create one of the very tools they would use in a survey of history. Instead of handing students a timeline, have them create one. But it should

not be just a timeline on paper which gets tucked away in a binder somewhere. Such paper timelines are fine, and they will eventually play a role in this learning activity. However, we need something bigger, something bolder, something more tangible than notebook paper, something that involves both individual creativity and class cooperative effort. Why not try creating a three-dimensional hanging timeline?

By creating this timeline, students gain ownership of it on several levels, as we shall see. By sharing their individual pieces of the timeline, students internalize the information and learn to look actively for the connections and relationships that exist among the timeline entries. The students are directly involved in all levels of this learning activity making the survey more relevant and more useful to the students. Furthermore, when it is finished, the timeline is a concrete product that students can be both indi-

When students believe the task they confront is valuable and will be appreciated by others, they inevitably rise to the challenge.

vidually and collectively proud, a product that can be viewed by anyone who enters the room, and a product that continues to serve as a valuable reference tool throughout the year.

We have found sufficient motivation and incentive among the students simply by stressing the significant value of the timeline along with the importance of their role in producing this entire project. When students believe the task they confront is valuable and will be appreciated by others, they inevitably rise to the challenge.

In this case, we challenge them to make three-dimensional representations of a person or event important to the historical period being surveyed. Depending on the class and the time available, the teacher should allow the students time to do some general research into the era and to brainstorm for potential timeline entries. A list of possibilities can be generated by the students. These possibilities should then be discussed and debated by the class as a whole to ensure that all entries are indeed significant to the timeline and the study focus. Individuals then select from this final list the topics that will become entries on the hanging timeline.

Clearly, allowing this process time to occur maximizes the amount of general knowledge that will be introduced to the class through student-generated research and discussion. It also maximizes the students' sense of both ownership and control over the learning activity that, in turn, creates vested interest, motivation, and a greater willingness on each student's part to expend the effort needed to create a quality product.

If time or circumstances do not allow for this process to unfold naturally, the teacher can abridge the project somewhat by creating in advance a list of possible entries. This is not the optimum procedure, and several cautions are in order. First and foremost, a high level of student involvement will be sacrificed, and along with that involvement goes a commensurate level of the students' sense of ownership and commitment. To ease this somewhat, the teacher must make sure the list of possibilities includes only persons and events truly significant to the larger focus of the class. Finally, the list must be large enough to allow every student real choices. If the last student to select a topic has only one choice, his or her interest and motivation may be severely limited.

Secondly, if the teacher creates the list, time should be taken to go over the list with the students. A brief discussion of each topic can spark interest and help students make choices. If possible, a little more time should be taken to allow students to do some general research on several topics from the list before they are asked to make their final choice. Once again, while the teacher must use his or her discretion based on the amount of time available for the project, the goal here is to give the students as much control as possible.

Once students have selected a topic, they must create a three-dimensional representation of the topic to be hung in the timeline. This entry does, however, have to meet certain requirements. First, each student must thoroughly research a topic and become the class expert on it. Students should be told from the beginning that this information is important to future activities, and they will be expected to share information about their respective topics whenever the need arises. In addition, descriptive information, as well as an identifying date and title, must be presented on the timeline entry. That way anyone examining the timeline can learn the significance of the entry even if the creator is not present to explain it in person.

Size may also be restricted. We use a roughly six-by-eight inch format because that allows us to fit two entries per student in the space we have for the timeline – a clothesline suspended a few inches below the ceiling and stretching across the entire length of our classroom. In our case, width is slightly more crucial than height because our older building has high ceilings. Consequently, we can be flexible, but we encourage all entries to remain within suggested guidelines.

Students also need to keep in mind the visual impact of their entry: it must be clearly visible from throughout the room. Hence, though space may require the entry to be relatively small, it cannot be too tiny. This causes the student to use more creative ingenuity in finding appropriate ways to design each entry. Finally, weight can be a consideration as well, depending on how you plan to hang your timeline. While it would be difficult to put an exact weight limit on the project, the teacher should point out to the students the need to be wary of potentially heavy projects. As work progresses the teacher can monitor this and avoid any weighty problems. We have yet to encounter a project that was too heavy, but I suppose there is always a first time!

With these few guidelines in mind, students research, design, and make their timeline entries. The results are always varied, unusual, creative, and interesting.

We like to make a special occasion out of hanging the entries. On a predetermined date, when all entries are ready, we borrow the custodian's rolling steps. Then, going in chronological order, each student stands before the class, shows and briefly describes his or her timeline entry, emphasizing the importance of the person or event to our larger studies of a watershed, and then ceremoniously climbs the ladder to hang the entry in its proper place along the timeline.

At the same time, students in the class create a paper copy of the timeline for their notebooks. They list by date, title, and significance each entry as it is presented and hung. They also include a small sketch of the project on their timeline. This provides each student with a personal record of the entire timeline to which he/she can refer when away from the classroom. Writing down the events uses hand-eye reinforcement of the learning and gives each student yet another motivation for listening to the presenters. Thus, in addition to the historical content, research skills, organizational skills, creative design skills, writing skills, listening skills, oral presentation skills, and note-taking skills are all integral to this learning activity.

Perhaps the most thrilling aspect of all is the unmistakable sense of proud ownership students demonstrate when they explain the hanging timeline to guests.

By the time all entries have been presented and hung, students have surveyed an entire period of history. They have also created their own ongoing research and study guide which serves as a constant visual reminder of chronological relationships as well as specific people and events important to our larger exploration of the watersheds in our region.

What is perhaps the most thrilling aspect of all, however, is the unmistakable sense of proud ownership students demonstrate when they explain the hanging timeline to guests or when their particular entry topic comes up in subsequent discussions. **ш**

American Diaries

Personalizing History

8.

*S*hhh . . .

Lights off . . . heads down, eyes closed . . . Shhh . . .

An early December morning, almost dawn. You pull the bearskin closer against the morning chill. The fire has died to embers, but thin wisps of smoke spiral upward to join the faint haze floating listlessly above you. Tiny ice crystals sparkle all over the silent, fur-wrapped forms of your sister and brother sleeping peacefully next to you – ice crystals, or maybe snowflakes that sneaked silently in through the small fissures in the bark skin of your wigwam during the night .

Muffled rustlings outside . . . deerskin moccasins, footfalls on a thin coating of new snow. Women of the sib (your clan) throw sticks on the cooking fires which flare back to life with loud cracklings and pops. Clay pots scrape across the cooking stones, a familiar sound at once grating and comforting. What else do you hear? What do you smell? What do you feel? What thoughts cross your mind as you awaken on this December morning four hundred years ago?

This sort of introduction helps me make the point that you have to be there! If *you* are there, then your readers will be there, too. If you're not there, your readers can't possibly get there, either. Grab those readers and pull them along with you!

That's what I tell my students whenever we start a new writing endeavor in WATERSHED. No matter what the topic, the writer has both the power and the obligation to make the words blossom into reality – a virtual reality, in contemporary parlance, that makes readers want to follow the writer wherever he or she may lead. To use this power effectively and to fulfill this obligation, the writer must first *be there* in his or her own mind.

In no assignment is this more evident or more useful as a learning tool than in the American Diaries activities. We use American Diaries in both our Sense of Time and our Sense of Quality phases as an enjoyable way to practice important writing skills while learning historical information about the various groups of people who have lived in our region. In addition, since this activity is not limited to a single writing exercise, it reestablishes the flow of historical eras so often lost in traditional history classes. At the same time, this ongoing activity serves as a secondary structural form for the class linking the historical groups we study to both the present and the future of our area. Furthermore, it allows the students significant control as they create the characters and the situations they will describe.

Our students write from seven to ten American Diaries during their year. In each, the student "becomes" a character living in this area during a particular period of our history. We begin, as did this chapter, with the native American Leni-Lenape who inhabited this part of the Delaware Valley for nearly 3000 years before Europeans arrived. The students write their first American Diary as one of numerous experiences, such as the Feast Day described in Chapter 4, centered on the Lenape. Students describe as vividly as possible a day in the life of a Lenape boy or girl around the year 1600, before the arrival of European settlers in our region. Students have to work in as many realistic details of Lenape life as possible while simultaneously creating credible characters and a suitable plotline. Thus, students have a great deal of freedom within the assignment while working on particular skills.

In addition, the instructions for each American Diary ask students to focus on specific writing skills. These change each year depending on observed needs of students, but they might include elements such as punctuating dialogue, using active verbs, or varying sentence structure. The teacher should select these emphases based on the needs of the individuals in the class, and students often assume the decision-making role as the year progresses. While the teachers determine the special attention areas in the first assignments, students begin to self-select them in later assignments. This helps them become better self-assessors – and isn't that the ultimate goal of education? Once again, this also provides students with a real sense of control and ownership over their work.

Here is a sample of the instruction cover sheet we use for all the American Diary assignments. While the specifics change in each, the format remains essentially the same:

AMERICAN DIARY

#3

LENAPE

Name:_____

Purpose:
_____ Imaginative / Narrative
_____ Sensory / Descriptive
_____ Practical / Informative
_____ Analytical / Expository

Audience:
General:_____
Specific:_____

Special Attention Areas:
Mechanical: Spelling and avoid "to be" verbs

Organizational: Chronological through the day, plotline

Stylistic: Descriptive imagery, effective use of dialogue

Content: Factual information about aspects of lifestyle

Date Due: _____

Assignment: Using information you have learned from our reading, our discussions and our trips, describe as fully and as clearly as you can a day in the life of a young Lenape living in this area around 1620. Use sensory details and effective dialogue to make the time, the territory, and your character come alive for your readers.

BE THERE !!

You may use this sheet for your preliminary notes; attach any extra sheets and rough copies as needed. Finally, when you are ready to submit your edited draft, attach it at the back, <u>behind</u> this sheet, and any other preliminary sheets.

Whenever possible, we try to link American Diaries together. For example, the next two American Diaries we ask the students to write involve the first Europeans to our area, the Swedes. As was described in the chapter on Create-A-Colony, the first of these describes a Swedish settler's experiences on the voyage from Sweden to America in the winter of 1638. The next one is a detailed account of that same colonist's first year in New Sweden.

Moving chronologically, the next American Diary depicts the life of a young Quaker, between 1680 and 1720. Students read about George Fox and William Penn. We visit a Quaker meetinghouse and learn about the lifestyle of those earliest Welsh Quakers who peopled Penn's "Holy Experiment." We look at actual diaries from that era written by local Quakers. Then students select a specific year and describe life in Pennsylvania at that time from one young person's point of view.

Next we tour a working grist mill built by a Quaker family in 1704. There the students get to open the sluice, feel the cool dampness as the water wheel begins to turn the grinding stone, and hear the loud racket of the gearing and the chattering damsel clanking its rapid cadence. These experiences provide the students with sensory data and background information for an American Diary describing the life of a miller's apprentice sometime between 1730 and 1770. No book could adequately produce the images and stimuli that these firsthand experiences provide. The students use these vivid experiences to make their characters and their American Diaries come alive. It is easier to "be there" when you have actually *been there*!

From the Quakers we move on to the American Revolution as it moved across our region. The students write an account of the Battle of the Brandywine from one of several points of view: it can be of a colonial soldier, a British or a Hessian soldier, or a local Quaker citizen living in the area that became the battlefield. Regardless of the viewpoint they select, students must present a historically accurate chronology of the battle. We learn about the battle through primary resources that include general officers' accounts of the battle and diaries of local citizens. The students also tour the entire battle area, see for themselves the vistas Washington's army saw from its defensive positions along the river, and follow the actual marching routes used by the British and Hessian attackers. Once again, these firsthand experiences enhance students' understanding of the events and simultaneously provide them with personalized sensory images they can use in their writing. This, in turn, makes the writing more lively and colorful for students as well as for their audiences. The writing experience assumes a layer of significance and a mantle of personal interest that lifts it out of the dull routine of academic exercise. Students begin to enjoy writing, an elusive fate devoutly to be wished!

The writing experience assumes a layer of significance and a mantle of personal interest that lifts it out of the dull routine of academic exercise.

From the Battle of the Brandywine we follow the combatants through the subsequent events of that autumn in 1777. Still using firsthand experiences and field trips, we trace Washington's retreat from the Brandywine, to the Battle of the Clouds, the Paoli Massacre, the Battle of Germantown, and the siege of Philadelphia. Ultimately, like Washington's army, we end up at Valley Forge. Here the students write their next American Diary, a letter home from Valley Forge.

The students select their colonial origin as they create a character, perhaps the same character who survived the fiasco at Brandywine. They see where their fledgling state militia was encamped at Valley Forge. They research the different experiences that arose from the differing locations, some more sheltered than others. They learn how different states supplied their troops in different ways and how that affected the soldiers. The Connecticut soldiers were prepared for the cold winter; those from South Carolina were not. All of these factors must play a role in their description of life at Valley Forge that winter. Fiction and non-fiction are thus merged into a meaningful and enjoyable learning activity. Students learn the facts of their history as they learn to use the elements of fiction to improve their writing.

After the Revolutionary War, students experience what life was like in an industrial village during the nineteenth century. Using the Hagley Museum, original home of the DuPont company outside Wilmington, Delaware, as a model, the students write about a day in the life of a young machine shop apprentice, a black powder worker, or a sister, mother or wife living in the factory villages.

Some years we augment this experience with another nineteenth century American Diary. This optional writing assignment details the experiences of a young immigrant arriving in our area between 1870 and 1900. The students research immigrant groups that arrived during that period to find out where they originated and why they came. The students then create a story in diary or letter format to illustrate what they have learned through their research about the immigrant experience. Many students select immigrant groups who represent their own heritage. This gives an added degree of significance to the project as the students interview their parents and grandparents to gain insights into their own families' experiences.

As students complete their study of our region in the Sense of Quality phase of our year, our students look to the future as well as the past. They select one of two options for their last American Diary entry. They can write a letter to the future, or they can write a diary entry for the year 2020. If they select the first option, they have to describe contemporary life, particularly as it relates to our use of the environment. If they select the latter, they have to imagine, based on current trends and conditions, what life will be like for them in the year 2020.

By year's end students have an anthology of short stories that surveys the sweep of history in our region. Rereading their own stories provides an excellent review of important historical content and helps students remember the chronology as well. In addition, the students can use the collection to evaluate how their writing has changed over the six months from the first American Diary entry to the last.

While I have described the entries we use in WATERSHED, the possibilities are endless. This learning activity can be applied to any or all eras and locations. The key is to let the writing be creative and informative, to build in firsthand experiences, and to try whenever possible to maintain links and continuity from one writing assignment to the next. The students learn to *be there*, and that lesson pays off in their comprehension of the content and in their writing skills.

Let the writing be creative and informative, build in firsthand experiences, and try to maintain links and continuity from one writing assignment to the next.

On the following pages is a sample American Diary written by a Watershed student. While Elaine is a talented young writer, as this diary entry shows, she was not unusual. Most of the students enjoy this type of writing so much that they put extra effort into it and achieve results not unlike Elaine's.

One year, to vary the project a bit, we asked students to restrict their diaries to no more than two or three typed pages. We further instructed them to think of these diaries as preparation material for a longer summary paper at the end of the Sense of Time phase. This longer paper would incorporate elements and characters from all the shorter papers and would require students to pull it all together more formally. This approach also worked well. In particular, it helped some of the weaker writers feel more successful as they could produce shorter papers and not feel like they had not done as much as the more prolific writers in the class. Either way, American Diaries always prove to be a powerful and a popular project for the students as they showcase their knowledge of history and their writing talents.

American Diary #4

The Grist Mill

By Elaine Johanson

January 22nd, 1712

Dear Diary,

Hello! Today is my first day ever writing in a diary, and I don't know what to write. Maybe I'll tell you about myself and my life so that we can get to know each other better. Then, when I describe things, maybe they won't seem so strange to you.

My name is Alice Evans. I'm twelve years old and a miller apprentice, even though I'm a girl. Father doesn't mind at all. "Girls or boys, they're all the same to me," he says, "If they can do the work then I give them the job."

My brother, Nathan, is 14 years old. He doesn't want to become a miller. I don't know what he wants to be. I don't even think that Nathan knows who he wants to be. Father wasn't too happy when he found out that Nathan doesn't wish to become an apprentice, but he claims that I'm as good. I like that, so I try my very hardest to live up to Father's expectations.

My father, William Evans, is the very best miller around. Everybody admires his great mill. I'm glad that I can take part of the credit, and I'm even more glad when Father says to the company, "I'm afraid that I can't take all of the credit. My daughter, Alice, helps with the mill, too."

I try not to feel too important when he boasts about how great I am, but I often have to run off to the great willow tree outside so that I can hide my smiles behind the wispy branches. Father isn't too fond of those people who consider themselves to be better than anybody else, so I try my hardest not to show how proud I feel. Only the willow tree knows how I feel, but now you will, too.

My mother, Eleanore Evans, is a wispy woman, thin and graceful as a weeping willow tree's branch. She had long, dark brown hair that she often has up in a bun. During my life, I have only seen Mother with her hair down three times. Once when she was very sick, once in the morning when she was pinning it up, and once when she was working and her hair fell from its carefully pinned position. Mother looks so different with her hair down, I hardly recognize her. I'm glad that she keeps it up all the time because that is how I remember her.

My best friend is my cousin, Emily Evans. Emily is the best girl in the whole world. She has long, dark brown hair and sparkly brown eyes that very often sparkle with mischief instead of excitement. Father often grumbles about her being a bad influence, but even Father has to admit that Emily is the kindest, sweetest, most fun person I could possibly come in acquaintance with. He grumbles, but his eyes tell a different story completely.

Jonathan, Emily's twin brother, is a bother and a bore. I don't like him at all because he's always teasing me and pulling at my braids. I have two braids, one on each side of my head, and he likes to yank them. I don't like to tell on him, but I often wish that I could. If only he would go away! Emily truly dislikes Jonathan, but they often think up schemes together. The two are a dangerous pair! I have been the victim of some of the schemes, and they aren't as funny to the one who this unlucky privilege has befallen as it is to those who think it up!

Now that I have introduced you to the people that I will mention in my diary, I will tell you about my life as simply as I can.

I was born on March 3rd, 1700. I am the eldest girl in my family. My younger brother and sister, who are five and four, are named after my parents, William and Eleanore. We call them Little William and Little Eleanore because sometimes we get the elder William and Eleanore mixed up with the younger William and Eleanore! So we call them Little.

We live in a house next door to the gristmill. Every morning I run off to the gristmill to help Father. He says that I am the best apprentice that a man can wish for. Once again, I must seek the willow tree so that no one but he can hear how proud I am. I hope that the willow tree does not pour my secrets to Father. The branches can talk, you see, and Father often has a sort of *knowing* smile on his face when I talk with him. Perhaps that is why he gave me this journal. Oh, I hope that he does not read it!

Father's gristmill is three stories high, made of stone and wood. Father only uses oak because otherwise the vermin eat away at the wood and it becomes weak. Oak is very hardy and the termites can't eat it easily. The gristmill greatly resembles a large barn, and if you can imagine a barn you can certainly imagine a gristmill!

The mill dam is also made of logs because they soak up the water and prevent flooding. Everybody in the community helped to make Father's mill, so the work of a thousand hands went into its building. Father always helps others because of the good deed that they did him.

The dam creates a millpond, which is very good for ice skating on during the winter! It is also a lovely place to fish in and watch birds. I have benefited from fishing and bird watching by the millpond, as have the many others who have come to relax by it. I can recognize almost all of the birds who live around this area, and I am an experienced fisher. I am not boasting, I am telling the truth. Even Father says that it is not boasting. It is true, so I tell it.

The pond is my favorite place, partly because it is so peaceful. I like to go rowing on it in Father's little rowboat. He taught me how to row, and it has proven to be useful for fishing because I can just row into the middle of the pond, drop my line, and come up with a fish before I even know what I'm doing!

The first time I ever went into the mill was when I was two years old. Father opened the sluice gates and the water came rushing in with a splash! The gears rumbled and the stones began to gnash with the most power I had ever witnessed! Even Father couldn't stop them with his body's force if he had wanted to!

The floor rumbled in the worst way and it was all too much for a little girl of two. I ran back to the house, wailing for Mama. As soon as I found her, I buried my face in her skirts and cried. Father laughed when he returned from the mill. I remember how mad I was when he laughed!

Now I'm not afraid when the water comes rushing in and the floor rumbles. I'm not afraid when the stones grind the grain with that horrible gnashing. I'm simply not afraid anymore. I have no reason to be. I have spent a good part of my life in a mill and I know everything about it.

For you, I will describe today in perfect detail so that you may get an idea of how my life is.

This morning, I awoke to the sound of Mother, singing as she prepared breakfast. Many people come for breakfast at the miller's and I always have to help serve. With a sigh, I pulled on my dress and apron and began to serve Mother's meal.

The men were hungry, I could see that. I served them as quickly as I could before running off to the mill to help.

"Hello, Pussy," I said as I stroked Pussy's head.

Pussy is our good white cat. She catches more rodents than any of the other miller's cats combined. As a result, she is sleek and fat but as gentle as a mouse. The only things that she is unkind to is the mice that squeak as they hurry through their tiny passages in the mill.

We have four other cats, Millie, Trussy, Trinnie, and Little Puss. They are all kittens of Pussy and none of them look anything like Pussy but Little Puss. Little Puss is a miniature version of Pussy and she catches almost as many mice.

Millie is a soft gray cat, fat and soft. She is not as good of a mouser as Pussy, but she is so soft and sweet that we all love her anyway. Trussy and Trinnie are tabbys, thin and sleek and almost as good as Pussy. The cats are wonderful and they keep the rodents away. Father doesn't know what he would do without them. Rodents. Horrors!!! They rip the bags open to eat the grain, and they get in places that they shouldn't be.

Today, the dresser was coming in to dress the millstones. That was when he cuts the grooves into the stones so that the grinding stones can give off heat by means of the grooves and the ground flour was pushed out. The constant grinding wore down the grooves very often, so we often had a dresser come in. This dresser was very experienced, and Father wouldn't trust anybody else.

The first time he came in was when I was five years old. We had had dresser's before, but this dresser was new in town and ready to begin a new business with the millers in our area.

After greeting each other, Father asked him to "show his mettle." Father inspected his hands and I peeked over his shoulder to see what was the fuss. Deep inside the skin of the man's hands were tiny pieces of stone that had flown up when he had been dressing the stones and embedded themselves in his hands. I thought it was dreadful, but Father seemed to be pleased and he agreed to let him dress our stones. I suppose that he did a good job because Father asked him to return in a few weeks.

I gave Pussy one last pat before beginning the day's work.

I went outside to clear the flume and millrace from anything that might be in the way. This was winter, so the task was not as fun as it was in the warmer months. I hurried to the flume and millrace and knocked off all the icy branches that had fallen into them. I did the boring task as quickly as I possibly could because it was very cold outside. As soon as all the debris had been cleared, I ran to do my second task.

I ran to the water wheel and banged until all the confining ice had fallen off of it. The ice came raining down onto me, giving me invisible bruises. The noise was quite loud and annoying and I finished that horrid outdoor task as quickly as I possibly could. Once the water wheel was fairly free, I ran inside the mill and slammed the door behind myself.

"Alice! Don't slam the door!" Father scolded.

"I'm sorry, Father. I won't do it again," I told him.

"Alice, you've told me that a thousand times and not once have you kept your word. Please remember," Father said.

"Yes, Father," I said.

I hurried off to do my third task, greasing the bearings. I picked up the fat and carefully spread it over the gears. It was a disgusting task that I didn't enjoy at all.

Today, Richard was coming to dress the millstones. Richard was Emily's father's journeyman. Richard is quite nice, and I really like it when he comes to dress the millstones. I always watch.

Richard came into the mill, holding an awl and a long, straight stick. After greeting us, he went to the millstones. He carefully measured the lines with his stick before pounding straight grooves into the lines by the sticks. Tiny slivers of stone flew up into the air and became embedded in his hands. This was, in fact, good since millers judged a dresser's competitiveness by the number of stones embedded in their hands. If there were many, it meant that the dresser was very experienced.

Richard painstakingly pounded the grooves into the millstones. I hung nearby, near enough to watch but far enough away to avoid the stones. After a long time, Richard finished. With a wave to me and a cordial farewell to Father, Richard left.

Once he left, I returned to my daily work.

I began to pour Farmer Hugh's grain into the hopper so that it could be ground. After I had finished, Father went outside to open the flume gates and the headgates. Once he did, the water would come rushing to turn the water wheel.

A light rumbling noise was heard. It quickly became louder and louder until it shook the entire mill. The water rushed to turn the wheel. With a loud groan, the wheel began to turn. The wheel turned the gears and then the runner stones. As the stones turned, the grain was ground.

I ran to unload and bag the ground grain that poured out of the shoot. Once a bag was full, I tossed the bag out of the door on the second floor and into Farmer Hugh's wagon.

The day passed slowly as we ground piles and piles of grain. Finally, after a hard day's work, I trudged home and into the fire-lit kitchen. Mother had prepared dinner and it was sitting on the table, warm and steaming and ready to eat.

After eating a hearty dinner, I slowly walked upstairs. I called a good night to my family downstairs before jumping into the chilly linen sheets that covered my bed. I snuggled down into the downy comforters and went to sleep.

As I was closing my eyes, I was mentally going through all the tasks I would have to perform the next day. However, I didn't spend too much time thinking because I had to prepare for the long day ahead of me.

Before I could finish thinking through my chores, I was fast asleep. **ɯ**

Newspaper Project

9.

Headlining History

Extra! Extra! Read All About It!
Student Reporters Score Scoop!

Another student-directed approach to survey a long period of history in a short period of time is our 19th Century Newspaper Project. This project involves numerous skills including historical research, writing, drawing and design, and oral presentation skills, to name a few. At the same time, though the performance outcome is delineated specifically, it still allows a great deal of room for student choice and control.

The performance outcome for this learning activity is a review of significant historical events and people presented in the form of a newspaper. The context is our Sense of Time phase, and we use this activity to study the nineteenth century.

We introduce the activity through a class discussion concerning characteristics of an age. We ask students to brainstorm about major events in the day's news and about areas of major emphasis in modern life. Though specific news items change from year to year, certain ideas seem to emerge every year. The concept of speed and the notion of "instant" frequently arise in our discussions – "fast food" and "instant replay" – along with references to the growing importance of computers in our lives. Needless to say, this results in lively discussions that help us begin to think in terms of characteristic mega-trends and simultaneously foreshadow our forthcoming discussions in the Sense of Quality phase of our study.

From this discussion we ask students to share their perceptions of the nineteenth century. Each year's class is different in its responses, but students usually have enough background experience to think of westward expansion and the Civil War, if nothing else. This part of the discussion works well if you allow small groups to brainstorm first, and then have groups volunteer their perceptions. Whether from groups or from individuals, ideas are gathered and grouped to form umbrella categories, or mega-trends, which help us characterize the nineteenth century.

It is important in these discussions that the students realize that we are generalizing on a very large scale, and that the act of generalizing entails certain pitfalls. Generalizations serve only as guidelines for historians, much as a hypothesis is a guideline for a scientist. The greater task comes in the act of substantiating the generalization or the hypothesis. Indeed, their upcoming research will involve the specifics to help either confirm or disprove the choices.

Clearly, the generalizations selected will vary according to the time period to which this activity is applied. For our survey of the nineteenth century, we focus on four major trends: *sectionalism, industrialism, immigration, and expansion.*

Students then receive an instruction sheet which details the outcomes expected for this learning activity (see p. 71).

As you can readily see, the project is multi-faceted and requires the students to employ many different types of skills. We spend whatever time we need, usually about twenty to thirty minutes or so, reading through the instructions with students and answering their questions. This includes introducing and explaining terms, and explaining the procedures we will use for research.

Research time and facilities will vary greatly from school to school; so each teacher must establish whatever parameters will work best in his or her own situation. We work closely with our school librarian on this activity. She and her assistants have copies of the project instructions, and we have agreed on specific times when our students will use the library. Depending on the class, and the librarian's schedule, we often begin the research portion of this project with group reorientations to the library in general and to those resources that will be of the greatest help to the students. These lessons are conducted by the library staff. They review the logistics and layout of the library. They go over procedures for accessing periodicals and reference materials. They provide instruction in the newest electronic/computer assisted resources. The librarians have also put on reserve for our students helpful materials from the shelves that might otherwise be in circulation at that time, and they point these materials out to the students as well. All this background prepares the students to make the most of their time in the library.

NINETEENTH CENTURY "NEWSPAPER" PROJECT

NAME:_____

Directions: Listed below is a three-year period of time from the nineteenth century. You are to learn all you can about major world and national events that occurred during that time period. Then you will present your research to the class in the form of a newspaper.

Your newspaper must contain four main sections: World News, National News, an Editorial, and Special Features. These sections must include the following items:

A. World News: At least three (3) articles covering important world events; a different event /article for each of your years. Events reported must be international in scope but must have had an impact on the U.S. Include at least one (1) map and one (1) illustration as part of this section.

B. National News: At least three (3) articles covering important American events; a different event/article for each of your years. Events reported must be national in scope but must have had some impact on our region. Again, at least one (1) appropriate map and one (1) appropriate illustration must appear in this section as well.

C. Editorial: At least one (1) editorial expressing your opinion on one of the events covered in your National News section. (We will discuss editorial writing in class.)

D. Special Features: At least one (1) article from each of at least two (2) of the following feature topics:

Arts and Entertainment

Science and Technology

Fashion

Farming and Business

Want Ads or Personals

Articles in this section should realistically reflect life in your time period.

Don't forget that your paper will need a banner (title) and an appropriate layout. Again, we will discuss these in class.) Your newspaper may be hand-written or typed, but all maps and illustrations must be your own work (no photocopies!!). You are limited to both sides of one 12" x 18" sheet of drawing paper.

Be creative! Have fun !!

Your years are _____ .   Your newspaper is due on _____.

Visits to the library to research time periods can then be scheduled as deemed appropriate to your teaching situation. We use some full group sessions, but more often we send small groups to the library for flexible periods of time. This puts less strain on limited resources and makes it easier for the librarians or one of us to help individual students.

During the several weeks we allot for this activity, other activities continue to occur in the classroom as well. In related activities, we ask students to bring in newspaper articles and editorials to analyze and discuss to ascertain appropriate newspaper forms and styles. We practice writing headlines, lead paragraphs, and thesis statements. We discuss issues such as editorial stance, statements of fact versus statements of opinion, the use of supporting detail, and methods for introducing quotes into articles. We also look at the layout of a newspaper, which articles are considered the most important, what information is in the banner of a paper, and more.

We are fortunate to have a great many resources in our classroom. These include useful books and periodicals we have gathered over the years, some videos, and some computer reference materials. With these materials students can devote time to research in the room while others use the library resources.

Clearly there exists in this activity many options for students and teachers. For example, the length of time covered can vary. We often use three years simply because that period allows thirty-six students to cover an entire century with a few years on either side to show historical continuity and perspective. Similarly, we limit the size of the paper primarily for display purposes. We suspend the newspapers from strings along the ceiling; that way each paper can be viewed from both sides. We only have so much ceiling space, however, and everyone's paper must be displayed. Limiting the size of the product also makes the student aware of the need to be brief and to the point. It further requires students to plan and use that limited page space carefully by using organizational and design skills.

...allow the student to explore the time period in question and to reach his or her own conclusions concerning what to include and how to include it.

Other areas that can be altered to suit particular needs include the number of articles required, the types of sections and features needed, the number and types of illustrations expected, and so forth. The basic idea, however, is to allow the student to explore the time period in question and to reach his or her own conclusions concerning what to include and how to include it.

Throughout the research and preparation phases of this activity teachers act as advisors and guides. We often suggest topics, and we often help students choose between topics, steering students toward the more locally significant ones. We help explain what they do not understand, and we direct them to resources appropriate to their ability levels. We help proof-read articles and editorials, and we advise them on design or layout issues. *The ultimate decisions in all these cases, however, remain in students' hands.*

Once papers are completed, students present their work to the class. They list chronologically the major events they selected, and they defend the selection by explaining the significance of the event in terms of the major trends. The class takes notes on each presentation, and, by the time all the papers are presented, they each have a fairly extensive timeline of important nineteenth century figures and events. As we go through the presentations, students and teachers alike point out relationships among events. We discuss cause and effect, for example, and we trace the flow of the major trends throughout the course of that century.

It is always a pleasure to see the pride the students take in their accomplishments. The papers are proudly displayed, and students relish their roles as authorities on particular events.

Of course, we read and review each of the newspapers. We do not, however, make any marks on the paper itself. Instead, we give students a separate sheet praising their accomplishments and noting any errors or omissions. The student can then correct any such problems before the project goes on display for all to see. Students tend to appreciate this for several reasons. For one thing, they have usually put a lot of time and effort into the paper: having it covered with correction symbols or comments can ruin its appearance. Additionally, it keeps their errors private and helps to avoid any possible embarrassment. Both of these notions confirm the worth of the students' efforts and maintain the positive nature of the learning experience. Mistakes become an avenue for accomplishment, not a pathway to pain.

Mistakes become an avenue for accomplishment, not a pathway to pain.

As always, we look for ways to tie learning experiences together. To this end, our students are asked to make a second hanging timeline entry based on one of the events from their newspaper (see Chapter 6). Thus the two projects reinforce one another as well as the continuum of history and the Sense of Time we are attempting to develop. This also extends students' sense of ownership and personal involvement in their history while adding to the cumulative enjoyment students experience. **w**

Wyeth Look-Alikes

10.

Art as an Avenue to Awareness

I s it real, or is it . . . ?

Imitation may be the sincerest form of flattery, but it is also an excellent way to learn. When you try to imitate some person or activity, you are forced to scrutinize every detail, every nuance that makes your subject recognizable and unique. While so doing, you learn a great many facts about your subject, but you also learn a great deal about process and quality as well.

The final product of this learning activity is a student-made imitation of a painting. Any artist, past or present, can be the focus, as long as an appropriate context is provided. We happen to use the Wyeth family of artists because they live and paint in the watersheds we study, but the context goes deeper than just this obvious local connection. The true context underlying this activity is the examination of processes which result in quality productions, the very aim and heart of education.

We use this project to introduce our Sense of Quality phase where the students explore the systems that affect the quality of their lives. This activity, focusing on the tangible works of a painter, demonstrates the importance of understanding the elements that comprise a system, but also the need to look at the relationships that interweave those elements to create a significant whole. In this particular case, that significant whole is called *style*, that quality which sets any individual's work apart from all others.

To introduce the activity, we show side-by-side slides of paintings by two different artists. The students, in small groups, are asked to list as many ways as they can to differentiate between the two paintings. Then, using student volunteers to act as recorders, we make a class list on the board of elements suggested by the small groups. As groups make suggestions, we discuss ways to group ideas, and we eventually create a list of basic elements or tools the artist manipulates to create the painting.

A key discussion point arises here: we simply ask the students *why are the paintings different if they use the same elements?* The all too obvious but often overlooked answer is the concept of conscious choice and purposeful manipulation. The artist has a goal in mind and intentionally selects the way to present the various elements to achieve that goal. Paintings, like essays, photographs, ballets, buildings, and water treatment systems are not accidental happenstances. They are planned out and executed through a series of decisions, the results of which are tangibly present. From these results we can work backwards to analyze the decision-making process and evaluate its effectiveness. In short, we can use the elements to judge quality.

Inevitably, this leads to meaningful discussions of personal taste versus aesthetic quality. This works particularly well if you use an abstract painting as one of your comparative examples. Students (indeed, many adults) have a difficult time seeing that abstract paintings rely on the same elements and are thought out and composed in much the same way as more conventional or pictorial paintings. Furthermore, as with all paintings, we do not have to *like* the results to understand and appreciate the elements and processes. However, understanding the underlying structure and philosophy enables us to refine and defend our personal preferences. It seems to me that this is a fundamental tenet of education and of life in general: we need to understand before we judge. Paintings illustrate this universal concept in a way seventh graders can manage and even enjoy!

The students select one of the three Wyeths, N.C., Andrew, or Jamie based on their own personal preferences.

Not coincidentally, the list generated by the class always matches quite closely the one on the handout we now distribute to the students. This handout asks the students to describe the use of these artistic elements in four paintings by the artist in question and then to describe that artist's style based on the way those elements are commonly employed. We have chosen to use four paintings because that works within our time frame. If time allows, more paintings could easily be required and would enable the students to make even better assessments of the artist's style. Similarly, the students select one of the three Wyeths, N.C., Andrew, or Jamie based on their own personal preferences.

Here is what our worksheet looks like. You can modify this form to fit your particular needs.

WYETH STYLE SHEET

Name:_____ Artist:_____

Definitions	1	2	3	4	Summary
Title and Date					
General Subject Matter					
Dominant Colors Used					
Dominant Shapes Used					
Amount of Detail Depicted					
Type, Size, Direction of Lines					
Use of Light: Source/ Degree					
Texture					
Compositional Shape Employed					

Describe in your own words how you can always tell your painter's work from that of the others.

The reader will note that the sheet also has a space for definitions of the elements. We arrive at common working definitions as a group based on the preceding class discussion, and we fill in those definitions together at this point. The students are also reminded that one of the paintings they analyze must be the one they elect to imitate. A time frame is established when the students are to explore works by all three artists, make their selections, and conclude their stylistic analyses on the sheets.

Sometimes we collect these sheets; sometimes we do not. We always spend time discussing the work in progress with each student at some point during the process, and we always check to see that the sheet has been completed. Most years, once the sheets have been completed, we have a class discussion to share and review the students' impressions and analyses.

The students are free to select their medium and their technique, but they know that they are trying to make their picture look as much like the original as possible.

With their analyses completed, the students begin working on their look-alike painting. Here the challenging fun really begins! The students are free to select their medium and their technique, but they know that they are trying to make their picture look as much like the original as possible.

As pictures are completed, we make a poster board mat for each one. We label it with the painting's title, the name of the original artist, and the student's name. The "framed" drawings are then displayed in our own mini-museum for all to see and enjoy. Needless to say, the students see this as a validation of their efforts. The students also get the chance to tell the class about the painting they chose before they write their self-evaluation.

As another enjoyable method of reinforcing their hard work, we visit the Brandywine River Museum, home to many of the Wyeth's paintings. The students use the structured visit as another opportunity to analyze the painters' styles and to look for relationships between the paintings and the region we study. Here is a worksheet the students use to guide them on their museum trip. [For purposes of space, the multi-page form is condensed on the following page.]

BRANDYWINE RIVER MUSEUM WORKSHEET

Name:_____ Date:_____

  I. As you tour the museum galleries, identify and describe your favorite painting by each of the following artists:
   - a) N.C.Wyeth.
   - b) Andrew Wyeth.
   - c) Jamie Wyeth.
   - d) Any other artist whose work you saw.

 II. Which of the paintings you analyzed on the style sheet did you find in the museum?

III. Based on the examples displayed in the museum, describe how the Wyeths' styles are:
   - a) Similar.
   - b) Different.

IV. Which of the Wyeths do you prefer? Why?

 V. Which gallery did you like the most? Why?

VI. Identify by title, artist, date and gallery a painting that shows:
   - a) Atmospheric Perspective.
   - b) Linear Perspective.
   - c) A Well-defined, Specific Light source.
   - d) A Smooth Texture.
   - e) A Triangular Compositional Shape.
   - f) "Photographic" Detail.
   - g) Implied Detail.
   - h) A Place You Have Been.

VII. How does the museum building, itself, relate to the paintings it contains?

When all is said and done, the students have a tremendous sense of accomplishment on many levels. Even those who don't think they have artistic ability tend to be proud of their picture. They are also pleased with their new abilities to discuss the elements of artistic style which many begin to apply to other art experiences, such as photography. Perhaps more than anything else, however, the students have deepened their growing sense of personal involvement in their learning. The students' feelings of involvement, control, enjoyment, accomplishment, and ownership all accrue through this activity. Believe me, there is no greater thrill than when a student at the museum calls out,

"Here's *my* painting!" ɯ

A Fantastic Voyage 11.

Exploring the Human Body

What do George Bush, Michael Jordan, and Cinderella have in common?

They have all undergone a truly fantastic medical procedure that cured them of some dire illness or injury and, at the same time, have thereby helped students better understand the systems that comprise the human body. Each of these personalities, along with many others, has been the subject of the human body essay we call *The Fantastic Voyage*.

Any of you over thirty will immediately recognize that title. It belonged to a story by Isaac Asimov and subsequently to a movie released during the Cold War era, starring Raquel Welch and Stephen Boyd. The basic premise of the story, and the one we have adapted to this project, involved shrinking a team of scientists and their special ship down to molecular proportions and injecting them into the body of a dying man who was of critical importance to the nation's security. The miniature team traveled through this person's body, encountering numerous obstacles along the way and eventually saving the scientist's life. Once the lethal threat was successfully eliminated, the team had to escape from the scientist's body before the miraculous shrinking process automatically reversed itself. As in most Hollywood endeavors, all ends well: the scientist lives, the nation remains secure from the threat of Communism, and the co-stars live happily ever after.

Impossible premise, you say? Corny treatment and sloppy science? Terrible special effects by today's standards? Sure, no question. But what a great way to have students learn about the human body. When you cannot schedule a real field trip, an imaginary one can do just fine. In addition, it provides another great opportunity for students to have fun while controlling what they learn and how they reveal their accomplishments.

* * * *

HUMAN BODY ESSAY PRELIMINARY WORKSHEET

Name:_____ Date:_____

1. Name the celebrity/person whose body and ailment will be the subject of your story: _____

2. Name and/or describe the ailment to be addressed: _____
    _____

3. List the five (5) systems you plan to experience in your travels through this body:
    a. _____ b. _____ c. _____ d. _____ e. _____

4. How do you plan to enter this person's body?
    _____

5. How do you plan to exit this person's body?
    _____

6. Use this space to describe briefly the opening circumstances for your story. For example, who you are and why you are involved in helping the celebrity overcome the ailment? How will you be miniaturized? When and where is your story taking place?

7. Using the human body outline below, **draw and <u>annotate</u>** the path of your journey in this story. Be sure to include the way you enter, the way you leave, the systems you travel through, major organs you encounter, and major events or problems you confront along your trip.

    (A full-page outline of the human shape would be here.)

As you can see, meeting these requirements calls on the student to learn a great deal about the workings of the human body. We employ multiple techniques to help them with this information gathering. For instance, we provide a structured worksheet for each of the nine systems. These worksheets, such as the following one, give the student study and research guidelines by asking questions designed to ensure all the important aspects of the systems are addressed. In addition, the worksheet essay questions provide practice for various portions of the Fantastic Voyage, and students frequently transfer parts of these mini-essays to their larger story.

Here is a sample from the circulatory system. The general format remains the same for all nine systems. Once again, the form has been condensed to save space. In reality the form would provide room for the students to write their answers on the sheet.

SYSTEMS WORKSHEET   [page 1]   Name: _____

CIRCULATORY DIGESTIVE ENDOCRINE EXCRETORY MUSCULAR

NERVOUS REPRODUCTIVE RESPIRATORY SKELETAL

   I. In your own words, briefly but precisely describe the purpose (function) of this system. What does it do?

   II. Describe how the system works.

   III. List the major organs of the system.

   IV. List the major diseases or dysfunctions of the system and their causes.

   V. Attach a diagram or chart relating to this system.

   VI. Answer the questions on the back of this worksheet.

CIRCULATORY SYSTEM WORKSHEET   QUESTIONS [page 2]

1. What is *your* **Blood Type**? _____

2. Blood vessels that carry blood away from the heart are called _____.

3. Blood vessels that carry blood back to the heart are called _____.

4. What is **Blood Plasma**?

5. Name the major function of the following:

   Red Blood Cells:

   White Blood Cells:

   Blood Platelets :

6. Name at least six things that the blood carries to and from the cells of your body: A. _____   B. _____

   C. _____   D. _____

   E. _____   F. _____

7. Name at least two other functions of the blood other than transportation:

8. How does exercise help the circulatory system?

9. ANSWER TWO OF THE FOLLOWING: What is a "stroke?" What is a "heart attack?" How does blood clot? How does Blood fight infections? What are the causes of high blood pressure?

10. Draw a diagram of the heart and attach it to this worksheet.

11. Describe the path of a blood cell through the heart. Include the left atrium, right atrium, left and right ventricles, pulmonary artery, pulmonary vein, and aorta.

The actual work on these handouts can be treated in a number of different ways depending on the needs of the group. We have on occasion required that the worksheets be completed by each student and handed in for correction; however, this is our least favorite recourse and one we try to avoid. This tends to make the worksheet an end in itself, reminiscent of the methods employed in traditional curricula. By so doing, it also takes some of the responsibility away from the students.

We much prefer letting groups of four students work together on the worksheets which we then go over cooperatively with the entire class.

Sometimes we make individuals or groups responsible for leading discussions on a particular worksheet; other times we select individuals at random to discuss specific questions. The process of reviewing these worksheets ensures that all the students have been introduced to all the materials and the necessary information they contain. The technique used for the review should, to the greatest extent possible, put the responsibility for learning and sharing that information with students. Often students come up with skits to demonstrate the information.

The technique used for the review should, to the greatest possible extent, put the responsibility for learning and sharing that information with students.

To augment these worksheets, we show videos, we share drawings and charts that the students make of systems and organs, and we create *Door Person*. This latter project is described independently in the next chapter. For now, suffice it to say that this is a cooperative class project which involves creating and assembling a three-dimensional, life-sized model of all nine systems put together correctly.

As I have stressed throughout this book, no specific content exists or is taught in isolation. In this case, writing and time management skills are practiced along with our study of the human systems. To do this we model the writing process through a series of steps. Pre-writing activities that generate interest and ideas include the aforementioned work on Door Person and the worksheets. We have also shown the old movie *The Fantastic Voyage* or a more modern movie, *Inner Space,* which also involves traveling inside another body. Both of these can lead to lively discussions of human anatomy, characterization, descriptive techniques, and literary license, just to name a few possible topics! What is more important, they generate a great deal of interest in trying to write such a story.

With this motivation and interest established, students select the personality about whom they wish to write. This can be any character at all.

We have had politicians, sports personalities, rock stars, television and movie performers, historical figures, and even cartoon characters. The students have complete freedom of choice.

Along with the character, students must select a malady, an illness, or an injury they will attempt to remedy in their story. Planning and continuity begin to play a role here as the students must select a malady that is in keeping with the personality selected. A baseball pitcher with an injured shoulder or elbow would make a good choice, for example; or a rock guitarist with a broken wrist. One student used Garfield, the cartoon cat, and cured its apparent eating disorder!

At this point the student begins to plan out how to cure the problem. In some cases a real cure exists. If such is the case, the student must find a way to incorporate that cure while simultaneously making necessary the miniaturized journey through the body. In cases where no cure exists, say AIDS or cancer, for instance, the student can make up a cure, but that cure should make some medical sense. To cure a case of cancer, for example, the student might develop a special laser that he or she uses to destroy cancerous cells in the body. While making these decisions, the students are encouraged to talk with one another and with the teachers to discuss possibilities and to compare ideas. Often students make wonderful suggestions to help someone else and, at the same time, get ideas for their own stories. These discussions also allow questions to be raised helping students direct their research into the human systems.

Often students make wonderful suggestions to help someone else and, at the same time, get ideas for their own stories.

Once students have made the three basic decisions outlined above, they have to think about the journey, itself. To do this, we ask them to submit a list of the systems and the organs they think they would like to visit. At first, this is just a general list, but we then ask them to put the systems and organs in the order they will be visited and to defend their choices with respect to both anatomy and their story. As part of this, we require that each student draw a body map showing the course to follow through the body. This technique helps students make informed and logical choices and ensures that they will not try to travel directly from the mouth to the heart, for example! It also helps them confront the literary concept of continuity in their plotlines.

These body maps and plot outlines are shared with other students and with teachers, all of whom make suggestions, point out potential problems or mistakes, and offer positive reinforcement of good ideas. The students rework their maps and their plotlines as necessary.

If you will forgive the pun: with this skeleton in place, students are ready to begin fleshing out their stories with appropriate details and descriptions. At several key points throughout this process we stop and compare results. We look at introductory passages, for instance, to see that the setting and the characters are adequately established. Later, we ask students to share descriptions of particular portions of their journeys, perhaps the passage through the heart or a pressure-filled passage through a Bowman's capsule in the kidneys. As noted before, many of these descriptions come, at least in a rewritten form, from the ancillary worksheets. In sharing these passages, students can work on correcting any content errors. They can also work on descriptive writing techniques, such as using all five of their senses in a paragraph. Both goals are viewed as equally integral aspects of the same larger goal – the ability to communicate knowledge of human body systems.

Eventually this end is achieved as the stories are completed. The students draw illustrations and make covers to develop artistic skills along with the writing. We share the stories with each other. This gives us one more opportunity to review the forms and functions of the systems and the organs in the human body and allows us one more chance to catch and clear up misconceptions or misinformation. This review also provides an avenue to introduce the next set of systems we will explore, our homes.

In addition to sharing and reviewing as a class, we put excerpts into our monthly newsletter, and we read some at the next open house. It is important to provide a use, or in this case an audience for students' productions. Students need to see their work published or presented to the world beyond their classroom. This validates their efforts and reinforces the sense that their academic performance and the real world are connected, a connection too often overlooked and lost in traditional curricula.

Students need to see their work published or presented to the world beyond their classroom.

Finally, students evaluate their own performance. They review the entire process and assess what aspects of the activity they found easy or difficult. They look for ways to apply what they have learned and for ways to improve their performance in the future. From the selection process through the writing process to the evaluation process, students have maintained most of the control over the learning experience. They have been able to answer questions and address issues of immediate concern to themselves, and they have had fun doing so. Granted, teachers must set some reasonable parameters and expectations, but students willingly accept them as guidelines, not limitations. Students' creativity flourishes and their individuality is confirmed and validated every step of the way. The activity becomes one more fantastic voyage into whole-learning. ɯ

Door Person

A Human Body Map

12.

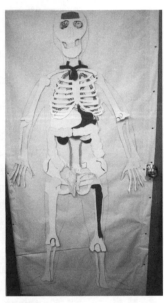

When it comes to introducing students to the systems of the human body, *no body* beats "Door Person!" Used in conjunction with the Fantastic Voyage essay described in the previous chapter, "Door Person" is always a clear favorite with the students.

Who is "Door Person," and where can you find this remarkable teacher? "Door Person" has many names and can be found hanging around the WATERSHED room during our Sense of Quality phase. "Door Person" can be found in your room, too; all you have to do is ask the students!

"Door Person" is a life-sized, three-dimensional map of a human body that students create as a way to demonstrate what they have learned about human anatomy. We have created "Door Person" in several different ways, as I will explain shortly; but the results have always been superb.

The first decision you have to make if you want to have "Door Person" come to your classroom is whether you want a single version or multiple versions. We have used both quite successfully. The decision might depend on how many materials you have available; it certainly depends on how much space you have. Assuming that most teachers face serious limitations in both materials and space, let's work with a single "Door Person" first, and then I can describe variations for multiple versions.

First you need a large sheet of paper or cloth. We have always used a six foot length of brown packaging paper, the kind that comes on forty-five inch wide, one hundred foot rolls. I am sure any craft or art paper which is fairly durable would work, as would an old bed sheet or a length of any plain colored cloth. The size and durability of the basic material are the crucial factors here.

Once you have your background material, you need a volunteer. This can be a student, you, a parent, your principal, anyone crazy enough to volunteer. We have frequently let our student teachers "volunteer."

Spread your basic paper or cloth out on a hard surface: a non-carpeted floor works best; a large table top would do if it is at least as long as your victim. The volunteer lies down on the paper with his or her arms and legs spread slightly, and the students trace the outline of the volunteer's body onto the background material. If you are working on paper, a pencil tracing is preferable to any sort of ink. The original tracing will be far from perfect, and glaring errors can be adjusted easily if the line is only penciled. Once amended, the line can be darkened with a permanent marker or paint.

So formed, "Door Person" is now hung in the classroom. We have found that a closet door works best for us, hence the name "Door Person," but any expanse of wall could do as well.

Next, the class is divided into groups. The size of the group is up to the teacher, but I recommend groups of two to five students. More than five students per group tends to preclude active participation by all students. We use four students per group; that number happens to work well for us because we generally have thirty-six students and we explore nine body systems. Again, the teacher can use fewer systems, or can subdivide systems to allow for more groups, depending on the class size, experience and focus.

At any rate, each group selects a body system. These groups become the class specialists in that system, much as doctors often specialize. Keep in mind, however, that we use this learning activity in conjunction with the worksheets and the Fantastic Voyage essay thus ensuring that students are learning about all systems. If you are using this project by itself, then you need to spend more time on the sharing phase toward the end.

Each group is responsible for creating its particular system for "Door Person." This involves initial research into the form and the functions of the system. It also calls for planning, creativity, and coordination among groups. This gives the students a great deal of control over the project. Much like the Fantastic Voyage described in the previous chapter, the outcome does not limit the students' creativity or sense of control. Nor do the following guidelines that help students plan their choices.

1. Systems and organs must be life-sized and accurately represented with respect to their location and interconnections.

2. The students may use any materials they wish. They may draw some systems or parts of systems directly on to "Door Person;" they may draw systems or organs on cardboard and then attach them to "Door Person;" or they may devise other more creative ways to represent the system. One of my recent favorites was the urinary portions of the excretory system which were created out of sponges and plastic tubing from our aquarium supplies. We have also found acetate to be very helpful, particularly in light of the next guideline.

3. All systems and organs must be visible. Consequently, groups must discuss their plans with other groups and work out ways to move systems aside to reveal underlying ones. To make this a little less cumbersome, we allow full body systems such as the skeletal, circulatory and muscular systems to be represented on only one half of the body. Still, groups must coordinate their efforts.

4. Each student in the group must participate in making the system. Furthermore, each student must also be prepared to answer questions about that system during our sharing and review discussions.

With these general guidelines in mind, groups are given time to work. This usually takes a period of two weeks or so, though that time is also being used for our work on the Fantastic Voyage as well. Nonetheless, "Door Person" begins to appear little by little as groups draw or attach the various systems to the basic form.

Because "Door Person" is visible to us all, coordination is virtually assured. Each group can see potential problems as they arise. Let's say, for example, that the skeletal system group tries to attach the rib cage before the heart and lungs have been properly placed. The circulatory and respiratory groups will be immediately aware of the problem and step in to stop the skeletal group from making a major error and to work out ways to ensure that "Door Person" comes together correctly.

Not surprisingly, the system that may cause the greatest problem is the reproductive system. First and foremost, there are the decisions each teacher must make regarding this system. Is it age appropriate to include this system? Do philosophical or curricular concerns prohibit its inclusion or discussion? If such problems exist, simply omit it. If it is appropriate, as we believe it is for our seventh graders, then I recommend that you require the group assigned to that system to represent both sexes on "Door Person." This always proves challenging, but never impossible. As with all the other systems and their coordination, the decisions and solutions concerning this particular challenge always come from students.

Once all the groups have completed their system, we convene as a class to share our efforts and evaluate our "Door Person." Each group is required to review the forms and the functions of the system it made, to explain the connections and relationships its system shares with other systems, and to defend the manner in which that system is represented on "Door Person." After each presentation, the class and the teachers ask any questions or make comments or suggestions in reaction to the group's production and presentation.

These presentations allow students a chance to show off their accomplishments and thus to achieve peer and teacher confirmation and acclamation for their efforts.

These presentations serve several important purposes which, by now, should be quite apparent. For one thing, they allow students a chance to show off their accomplishments and thus to achieve peer and teacher confirmation and acclamation for their efforts. In addition, by teaching the class, each group further internalizes the information they garnered as they researched and constructed a particular body system. Furthermore, the class experiences yet another opportunity to review all the systems of the body in an enjoyable and student-directed manner. Finally, "Door Person" remains in the room for the remainder of the year and becomes a student-produced resource to which we continually refer in our subsequent study of house and regional systems. This, again, adds to the students' sense of ownership and their sense of pride which reinforces the entire learning process. As I mentioned previously, if this activity is being used by itself, the teacher will probably want to spend a longer period of time on this sharing and review phase to ensure successful internalization of the information covered.

By now I am certain that teachers reading this have imagined innumerable ways to vary the learning activity to suit their particular needs. One easy way to do this, which I alluded to earlier, is simply to allow for multiple "Door Persons." To do this, the class is again divided into appropriate groups, but each group makes its own tracing and develops all of the systems for its own "Door Person." The advantage to this variation, obviously, is the way it requires each group to work with all the systems. It has some disadvantages, however. For one thing, it alters the levels of co-operation needed to make the "Door Person." Clearly cooperative skills are still required, but only within the smaller group, not the class as a whole. Similarly, while each group achieves a sense of accomplishment (perhaps even a slightly greater sense) by making an entire "Door Person," the class loses some of its unified sense of group achievement. Finally, on a very practical level, storing and displaying multiple versions of "Door Person" can cause numerous logistical problems which might outweigh the benefits. Nevertheless, if space and materials are not a problem, this remains a viable alternative. We have had success with both methods.

As always, the entire process is topped off with a reflective student self-evaluation. Students assess their individual performance, that of their group, and that of the entire class as well. The teacher, of course, has been circulating throughout this process, noting strengths and weaknesses of individuals and of groups. Generally these are discussed immediately with the students; some are also discussed or described further in our narrative reviews of the students' progress and accomplishments. Either way, as numerous skills have been developed or honed in a whole-learning activity of this sort, there is never a shortage of areas to praise or of suggestions for future improvement. ɯ

House Design

Dreaming, Drawing, and Decision Making

13.

Everyone loves to dream. By definition, all dreams contain elements of fantasy. Consequently, they usually are enjoyable and frequently relaxing experiences – playtime for the mind, so to speak. Yet, all dreams are grounded to some degree in the dreamer's experiential reality. That reality forms a context for the dreams and establishes certain limits or parameters of the dream. If these parameters are pushed too far away from the basic reality, or if they are exceeded by the dreamer, we see that dream as pure fantasy with little significance beyond its recreational impact. When these parameters remain firmly rooted in reality, however, dreams and the imagination become the seeds of progress and change of learning. This is why tapping into students' imaginations can be such a powerful resource, particularly when that power is directed toward a basic human reality such as the need for shelter from the elements.

We all need a home. Whether it is a mansion estate or a cardboard box, we all need shelter from the vagaries of nature and society. We all need a place to call our own. Furthermore, we each have dreams concerning this place and the way we would most like it to be. Indeed, consciously or unconsciously, our definition of this place is intimately tied to our sense of personal identity and to the role we have in society and culture. A home and the systems that comprise it are fundamental elements that help determine the quality of our life. Our students are no different in this respect. They are drawn easily into discussions about their notions of a home. It is a topic they all love to discuss, and they react positively when presented with the opportunity.

Exploring the concept of this place is an excellent way for students to apply their imaginations to help foster their understanding of themselves and of their society. They can have fun while grappling with and learning about very real issues that affect them throughout their life. This house design activity allows them to learn countless facts, to experience innu-

This house design project is a whole-learning opportunity at its best, with all the necessary components to make for an enjoyable and memorable experience.

merable concepts, and to practice an unlimited range of life skills. What is more, it allows them an opportunity to create a dream. They have the motivation and the interest, and this project provides them with clear amounts of control. When completed, the students have a tangible product, as well as new skills, in which they can take pride. This house design project is a whole-learning opportunity at its best, with all the necessary components to make for an enjoyable and a memorable experience.

The performance outcome of this particular dream will be multi-faceted. As the following instruction sheet indicates, the project includes several types of drawings: a written component, an oral presentation, and a scale model of a house that students design.

HOUSE DESIGN PROJECT

You and your group are to design a house for a "family" of four persons with a family income of about $75,000 per year. The house is to be "built" on a plot no greater than one acre in area. You may choose where it will be located, but you will need to account for climate and land conditions.

The final project will include:

- a "preconstruction" plot diagram to show the size, shape, topographic features, and compass orientation of the land.

- a "post-construction" landscaping diagram to show how you fit the building into its environment

- floor plans, including heating/cooling and electrical considerations

- a frontal and a side elevation

- an optional model built to a $1/_4$ inch = 1 foot scale

- a brief written summary, or sales pitch, describing the house and any of its special features.

GOOD LUCK AND HAVE FUN!!!

We usually begin the activity by asking small groups of students to develop lists of the necessary characteristics of a home. Students usually have no trouble listing types of rooms, a roof, doors and windows, along with facilities for utilities such as water, heat, and energy. As we share these lists, we question the purpose for each suggested item: why do we need it or what purpose does it serve? How does it improve the quality of our life? This usually leads to some lively discussions over degrees of necessity. Such discussions are wonderful opportunities for students to hear alternative perspectives on the definition of a home.

Ultimately, students are grouped and receive the project instructions. The grouping process can be of their choosing, or it can be assigned; the teacher must use his or her discretion based on the group. I prefer to allow students to select their own partners, but I have experienced situations where it was necessary or preferable to engineer the teams.

Similarly, the pretext for the groupings can vary. We have often created teams as "families" designing their own houses. We have also been very successful forming teams as architectural companies designing houses for a development. This latter approach makes it easier to account for why everyone is using the same land and the same requirements. It also makes peer assessment easier. Each team must present its plans to the builder, the class as a whole. The builder has set the requirements and is seeking plans for several different models within those parameters. Once the partnerships have been created, we go over the instruction sheet as a class. This gives everyone a chance to hear the requirements and ask questions.

If we use the architectural firm approach, we ask the group to use the following form to determine responsibilities within their company. This helps the students make more efficient use of time, talents, and preferences. It also makes individual responsibilities quite clear to everyone so the group can hold its members accountable for the success of the whole. Later, when we assess the projects, it allows us to review the specific contributions of each student.

The mini-groups then begin to work on their project by discussing with each other what each feels his/her home should be like. This is an ongoing process of give and take, a very realistic situation where each student must recognize the wishes of the other and find ways to accommodate all parties. The process still allows them a great deal of latitude, though in teams they still control the decision-making process.

While this process occurs over a period of several days, class time is used to present several important lessons that assist students with their larger

HOUSE DESIGN PROJECT

Architectural Firm Project Record Sheet

Name of Firm: _____

List Partners: _____   _____

_____   _____

_____   _____

While the entire firm assumes ultimate responsibility for the design and completion of this project for the client, the individual partners will be held accountable for the following aspects of the overall project.

A. Drawing Floor Plans: _____ Primary

_____ Assistant

B. Drawing Elevations: _____ Primary

_____ Assistant

C. Drawing Landscape

Components: _____ Primary

_____ Assistant

D. Artistic Rendering: _____

E. Arranging Display: _____

F. Writing Presentation: _____

G. Presentation: _____

task. Two types of lessons are particularly important and deserve special description here. They are 1) lessons designed to help students with the financial aspects of the home, and 2) lessons concerning architectural drawing and considerations.

Since my experience is limited to a relatively affluent area, I have found my students to have a particularly difficult time with the idea of a budget. In seventh grade, at least in my school district, students seem to have very little concept of what things cost in the real world. Without diverging into the socioeconomic factors that may cause this phenomenon, suffice to say that they have a tremendously inflated image of what real people earn and what they can afford. By national statistical standards, the $75,000 gross family income we allow is quite generous. By local standards, it is less so. It was set as an obvious compromise between the national average household income and that of our region. The teacher should determine the figures to use based on the region where the students live.

Teachers should change the number of people in the household as well if they deem other conditions more appropriate to their students. It should be noted here that we establish a number of persons in the household along with the total group income, but we do not assign any roles or ages to those people. The size of the household forces the students to consider more budgetary and design concepts than they would have to if they were planning a home for a solitary individual. However, it does not presuppose any particular family structure.

At any rate, we begin working on budgets by having small groups cooperate to make up lists of household expenditures. How does a family spend its income? We pool our lists and merge related suggestions into suitable categories to create a class list that covers as many pertinent types of expenditures as we can. While each year's class determines its own unique wording, the general class list always ends up including areas such as a mortgage, food, clothing, transportation, communication, utilities, various insurance costs, dental and medical expenses, recreational considerations, and taxes. We have also had lists that included categories such as furnishings, home maintenance, gifts, charitable donations, pet supplies, education, and savings or investments. Clearly, there is room for a wide variety of responses. The important point here is that the class discuss as many types of household expenses as possible and determine as a group what should be included on the master list. Note that even here students have control through consensus over the categories that ultimately end up on the class list.

We next challenge students to prepare a monthly household budget based on the gross household income and these expense categories. To do this, students have to do a little research at home. What does electricity cost? How much does their family spend a week on groceries? Check the paper and see what an automobile costs. Questions such as these help students get an idea of real world conditions. The teacher should keep in mind that we never ask the student to divulge the specifics of this information to the class. That should go without saying. We want the student to use this information to formulate his or her own conclusions about a hypothetical budget. Ultimately, these budgetary decisions impact on the amount of money they will have to build or buy their home.

HOUSE DESIGN PROJECT

BUDGET WORKSHEET

Name of Architectural Firm:_____

GROSS "Family" Income = $75,000 per year. <u>No extra income will be counted!</u>

Combined Taxes = 30% [Multiply .3 x $75,000] = $ _____

NET "Family" Income = $75,000 minus Combined Taxes = $_____

NET MONTHLY = Net divided by 12 = $_____

<u>MONTHLY BUDGET</u>

<u>Budget Category</u>	Amount Budgeted
FOOD	$_____
CLOTHING	$_____
TRANSPORTATION [$400 per auto]	$_____
UTILITIES / SERVICES	$_____
OTHER	$_____
OTHER	$_____
OTHER	$_____
OTHER	$_____
OTHER	$_____
Subtotal	$_____

Monthly Housing Budget = Monthly Net <u>minus</u> the Subtotal = $ _____

Into this budgetary process we interject a few givens. For example, to keep things relatively simple for seventh graders, we instruct them to deduct 30% of their gross annual income as payment for all types of taxes. We discuss what these taxes are: various federal, state, and local income taxes, real estate taxes, and so forth. We do not, however, expect them to go through each of these taxes and determine specific amounts that are withheld. With older students, particularly students who draw a real paycheck, this would be a more worthwhile exercise. For our students, we do not need that level of sophistication; we simply need for them to realize that there is a distinct difference between gross and net incomes.

Similarly, we use local information to establish a uniform mortgage rate for the class to use. We go over the formula for determining simple interest, a process which is reinforced by the math teacher as well. We place a limit on the amount of money the students have for a down payment. Though they moan and groan, we do not allow any group additional money from state lottery winnings or the timely demise of a rich spinster aunt. This keeps all groups on a relatively even plane that better allows them to compare their results later in the project.

HOUSE DESIGN PROJECT

BUDGET WORKSHEET page 2

Name of Architectural Firm:_____

PLANNED HOUSING COSTS

Category	Monthly Cost	Number/Cost
Basic House		(includes 30 year fixed mortgage at 8%, real estate taxes, and insurance escrow)
	= $700 per month per 1000 square feet	_____
Fireplace	= $63 per month each	_____
Spa	= $63 per month each	_____
Swimming Pool	= $168 per month	_____
Deck/Patio	= $ 15 per month per 100 square feet	_____
Garage	= $42 per month per auto space	_____
	Total Monthly Cost =	_____

Many decisions remain in their hands, however. For example, once the financial restrictions are established, students can select the location for their home, the size of their plot of ground (up to an acre), and the type or style of their home. Some years we have limited this to sites within our watershed area.

Before making these decisions, we encourage students to read the real estate pages of the local paper to see what type of price buys different types of homes. Comparing this information to their own hypothetical budget allows them to see what possibilities exist and what different features are commonly available. I usually collect multiple copies of real estate magazines, the kind you often find free for the taking at grocery stores. I have them on hand in the room for students to use.

The second area where students need guided help is the area of architectural design considerations and drawing techniques. This we accomplish using a combination of individual discovery and group sharing activities. At the start of the project, along with the basic instructions, each student receives the following three worksheets. Again, space has been saved here by condensing these forms. Feel free to add or delete rooms in keeping with your area's typical home.

HOUSE DESIGN PROJECT
WORKSHEET 1

Name:_____

Measure the size of the following rooms in your home:

ROOM	LENGTH	WIDTH	AREA IN SQUARE FEET
Living Room			
Dining Room			
Kitchen			
Family Room [den]			
Bedroom 1			
Bedroom 2			
Bedroom 3			
Bathroom			
Powder Room			
Hallway			
Closet			
Staircase			
Garage			
Other			

HOUSE DESIGN PROJECT
WORKSHEET 2

Name:_____

1. Measure the width of the front of your home: _____ feet

2. Measure the width of one side of your home: _____ feet

3. Measure the floor to ceiling height of at least three rooms:

    a. _____ ft.   b._____ ft.   c. _____ ft.

4. Locate a place in your home where you can measure the thickness of

    a. an EXTERIOR WALL _____ inches

    b. an INTERIOR WALL _____ inches

5. Measure the width of your driveway: _____ ft.

6. Measure the width of a sidewalk: _____ ft.

7. Make note of the locations of external faucets and outlets. What determines their location? Why do you think they are placed as they are? Would you change their location? Where and why?

8. Make note to yourself of external lighting features. Why have they been placed where they are? Would you change them?

HOUSE DESIGN PROJECT
WORKSHEET 3

Name:_____

Directions: Use a tape measure or yardstick to find the applicable dimensions of these basic items in your home. Put all your measurements in inches.

ITEM	WIDTH	HEIGHT Overall	HEIGHT From Floor	DEPTH From Wall
Front Door			X	X
Room Door			X	X
Window				X
Kitchen Counter	X	X		
Kitchen Sink		X		
Stove / Range		X		
Dishwasher		X		
Washer or Dryer		X		
Bathroom Sink		X		
Bathtub / Shower				
Toilet	X			
Garage Door			X	X
Stair step				
Bed		X		

These worksheets encourage students to explore their own homes and measure various important features to give themselves a realistic view of relative sizes. As you can see from the copies here, these sheets ask students to measure doorways, for example, stair riser heights, hallway widths, various room sizes, and the dimensions of appliances and fixtures. These sheets are optional: the student may do as much or as little of the sheet as he or she wants. We do not collect these worksheets; they are strictly for the student to use as personal reference data. We do tell them, however, that they should not come to us later on and ask how wide a door should be, how deep a kitchen counter is, or any other dimension that they could have discovered for themselves by using these sheets! Similarly, we will expect to see realistic sizes on their finished designs.

In addition to these optional worksheets, we show students samples of plot diagrams, floor plans, and elevations. We go over these examples to answer general questions and to point out important features. These samples remain posted in the room for continued reference.

We also spend some time drawing the various architectural symbols the students will need. We show them basic symbols for walls, doors, sliding doors, double hung and plate windows, stairs, plumbing and electrical fixtures, and so forth. We also elicit suggestions from the group, usually for more unusual items: recessed doors, fireplaces, garages, and other types of windows for example. As we draw each item on the board, students draw it as well on graph paper. They keep this record for future reference. If you do not feel comfortable with this aspect of the project, it could be a great opportunity to enlist the aid of a guest speaker. Perhaps your technology teacher or your art teacher has a background in architectural drawing. If not, perhaps a parent is an architect who would be willing to come in for an hour one day and show students how to draw these simple elements. As always, have the students make the invitation and host the guest; this adds to the overall impact of the whole-learning situation.

As we are going over these symbols, we also discuss design considerations such as private and public spaces in a home, traffic patterns, and the relationship between sizes of objects in the home and the proportions of the human body. Similarly, we discuss design needs relating to the regional topography and climate. One does not usually have a basement near the seashore or in areas with a high groundwater table, for example, just as one does not usually build a flat-roofed building in a region that experiences heavy snows. We also talk about types of heating and how each sort can influence a building's design, and the basic design of a plumbing system; and we even discuss passive solar heating and natural cooling techniques

107

based on landscape design and appropriate orientation of the building. Finally, we describe local ordinances and building codes when appropriate or necessary.

These class discussions are designed to help students consider as many realistic factors as possible as they design their ideal home. We try to limit the discussions at any one time, and we often wait to have them until a question or concern from students arises to initiate the discussion.

Along with all these pertinent discussions about various relationships, we go over scale and proportion. Students need to be able to convert actual sizes to the scale we have established for the project. We use a one quarter inch = one foot scale. This is large enough to allow for sufficient details while being small enough to keep the plans and the models manageable.

The majority of our time, however, is given to students to work on their designs. We circulate among the pairs to help with questions, review symbols, point out potential problems, and so forth. We suggest that the students work on a rough copy of their floor plans first with a final copy submitted only after initial problems have been corrected on the rough draft. Given the number of errors and changes students make from the moment they start their design to the moment they complete it, most students willingly take this suggestion seriously.

The final plans must include plumbing, electrical, and heating plans. Over the years we have experimented with different degrees of complexity depending on the level of sophistication we felt the class could handle. Sometimes we have requested to see wiring and heating pathways. Other times we have asked merely to see the locations of outlets, permanent light fixtures, and radiators or vents. The teacher must determine the level of sophistication required, keeping it to a level that will not frustrate the students. Always allow students to go beyond that level, however, and encourage them to do so.

With respect to plumbing, we have always required a bit more detail, probably because our WATERSHED focus is on water systems! Students must show us the water main entering the home, the water heater, the cold and hot water lines, the plumbing fixtures, and the waste water lines. All of this utility work, regardless of the complexity requested, is done on acetate sheets or tracing paper that students place over their basic floor plans. This allows us all to view these systems more easily, sometimes one at a time, and it enables students to draw and alter these systems without damaging their floor plans. When put together with the floor plans, the plot diagrams, the elevations, the drawings and the short written description, these overlays complete a very impressive package. Students are justly proud of their efforts, and they love to share their designs with anyone who will listen!

Students are justly proud of their efforts, and they love to share their designs with anyone who will listen!

Once the final designs have been submitted and reviewed, and once any last changes or corrections have been made, some teams begin to build their models. We require that the model be in the same scale as the drawing. This makes it much easier for students to build, because all the measurements are already there. It also makes it easier for them to see exactly how their design translates into three dimensions.

Students are free to experiment with building materials. We recommend and provide 8-ply poster board. Experience has shown it cuts easily, its thickness approximates the scale of the building, it can be curved and bent easily for unusual effects, it can be readily glued with either hot glue or white glue, and it makes a strong, yet light weight model. Some students, however, like corrugated cardboard; others prefer to use special styrofoam sheets they buy at local hobby shops. If students want these other materials, they have to provide those materials themselves.

Along with the elevations drawn by the students, the models occasionally surprise the students. What they thought looked good as a floor plan may sometimes leave something to be desired esthetically when viewed in three dimensions. Students are often pleasantly surprised to see how good their concept looks in reality.

Whether the design lives up to the dream or not, the project is always successful. Students learn a great deal about many realistic concepts and relationships. In their review and self-evaluation of this project, students always find much that they can point to with pride. They discuss aspects of the project they found difficult as well as what they learned through constant problem solving. This knowledge will certainly help them in other aspects of their lives now and in the future.

Even more, the students have seen once again that dreaming can lead to wonderful accomplishments – and that is the joy of learning that keeps minds actively engaged in the pursuit of knowledge! **w**

Adopt-A-Guest

14.

Inviting the World into the Classroom

But, Mr. Springer, they won't answer us; we're just kids!

They're people just like you and me. You never know until you try. Besides, what's the worst that can happen? They'll decline your invitation. No harm, no foul, and you'll still learn a whole lot in the process!

In fact, few learning activities offer so many potential rewards for such a minimal investment in time and effort. That's why Adopt-a-Guest is such a great activity. What is more, any student can do it, anywhere, and reap these same benefits.

I like to use Adopt-a-Guest as a year-long project; one that can be completed at any time. For one thing, this gives the student a major degree of control over the activity. Equally important, it allows potential guests more freedom for scheduling visits at their convenience and thus spreads guest speakers out throughout the year. But perhaps I am getting ahead of the story a bit. Let's go back and fill in the basic details.

Adopt-a-Guest, as its name implies, involves having each student select a person who has a real world vocation or avocation related to some aspect of the class's studies and the student's interests. The student finds out as much as possible about this person and then writes a letter asking if that person would share his or her expertise with the class. The person can be just about anyone, a parent, an acquaintance, a person featured in the local paper, or someone whose name surfaces in students' research on other learning activities. Though we have developed lists of names over the years, the students always come up with numerous candidates on their own. There certainly is no shortage of possibilities! We have had parents representing interesting occupations: doctors who addressed issues about human body systems, and parents with interesting hobbies like insect collecting and wilderness canoeing. We have had local professionals, such as the developer who planned and built the tallest buildings in Philadelphia. He visited and talked to the class about regional planning. We have had local artists, photographers, scientists, and historians from nearby businesses and universities who came in to shed light on various aspects of our regional studies. The list of possibilities is endless. We have even had students write to famous people such as Andrew Wyeth. The only requirement is that the person must have something worthwhile to add to the class's focus.

The student is responsible for all correspondence with this individual, beginning with a suitable letter of invitation. This letter must introduce the student, the class, and its topic to the person. The letter must also explain why the student thinks this person would be a good guest speaker; that is, explain how this person's area of expertise is related to the class's work. Finally, the letter politely asks the person to consider becoming a guest speaker in the classroom and offers the student's assistance in arranging any details to make the person's visit possible.

In Adopt-A-Guest the results are tangible and significant – the student receives a response from a real person in the real world, and that response requires further actions.

The reader will note that several important levels of learning occur as this process unfolds. Some research and analysis are involved in the selection of a potential guest. The larger skills, however, are those of communication and organization. The student has to write an acceptable letter to a distinct audience for an expressed purpose. This letter, however, has importance beyond just the act of letter writing. I remember learning to write letters in junior high school. We had a sample in our grammar book, and we had to make up a fictitious letter using that sample format. I am sure many of you recall a similar exercise. Our letters went no further than the teacher's desk, however. The end product was a grade, quickly forgotten, right along with some of the details of letter writing. In Adopt-a-Guest the results are tangible and significant: the student receives a response from a real person in the real world, and that response requires further actions.

In the event that the person cannot be a speaker, a follow-up thank you note is still in order. Thus the letter writing skills are practiced once again, still in a meaningful situation. If the person accepts the invitation, then the student must help make all the necessary arrangements. This can involve writing additional letters; often it also entails phone conversations. Either way, the student takes on the responsibility for scheduling the guest's appearance and for advising the guest on an appropriate focus or topic for his or her presentation to the class. This means that the student must know enough about the individual's interests, as well as about the class's work, to ensure a suitable match. Furthermore, the student must practice his or her communication and organizational skills under real world conditions. The results will be far more rewarding than a grade at the top of a piece of notebook paper.

Once all the pertinent arrangements have been made, the student completes his or her research on the guest speaker and prepares a short pre-visit introduction for the class. In this short presentation the student explains who the guest will be and describes the topic of the guest's talk. The student suggests aspects of the topic that will be particularly interesting or important, and recommends types of questions the other students might consider in preparation for the guest. The student takes on a leadership role, and the class receives a context for the experience.

When the guest arrives to speak, the student assumes the role of host or hostess. This involves greeting the guest, usually at the main office, introducing the guest to the teachers, showing the guest around the room and explaining what the class is presently studying. The student also introduces the speaker to the class when the presentation is about to begin.

When the speaker has finished his or her presentation, the student publicly thanks the speaker. The student then escorts the speaker out, helping, if needed, to carry any materials the speaker may have brought.

Two last writing tasks remain for the student. First, a thank you note is required. Along with expressing the class's gratitude and that of the individual student, this note should make specific reference to some aspect of the speaker's presentation the student found most interesting or informative. This is a great writing exercise that carries with it important lessons in social etiquette.

The last piece of required writing is the student's self-evaluation of the entire process. As always, the student describes what he or she has learned through this experience, what parts were difficult or easy, and what steps he or she will take to improve in the future.

As you can see, when repeated by multiple members of the class, this project benefits both individuals and the entire class. Individuals practice numerous communications skills; the class gets the opportunity to learn from a variety of real world figures. Tangentially, the school generally benefits as well. For one thing, it garners positive publicity generated by these guest speakers. We often inform the press and the community when a person is coming in to speak. This places both the speaker and the school in a positive light. Furthermore, other members of the school community can learn from the speaker. When we have a guest speaker, we invite parents and other interested people to come to the class and hear the presentation as well. Thus, everyone benefits.

...when we give students this responsibility, we tell them clearly that we think they are capable of interacting with the adult world.

What is perhaps most important, the activity, except for the initial idea, has been entirely under student control and direction. Students decide whom they wish to invite based on their own interests. Students make the contacts, the arrangements, and follow through as hosts. Students take the credit for the success of the activity and the learning involved. At every step students have been self-motivated by the thrill of working with "important" people. Furthermore, when we give students this responsibility, we tell them clearly that we think they are capable of interacting with the adult world. At a time when they are struggling with that very issue, our confidence in them, demonstrated simply by making the assignment, goes a very long way in building their self-confidence. That increases their desire to succeed in order to prove that our confidence was well placed. When they receive responses from their adopt-a-guests, the students thrive on the realization that the adult world recognizes them as valuable young adults.

Though this whole-learning activity requires very little effort on our part as teachers, indeed, perhaps the least effort of any of the activities described in this book, it yields the greatest rewards for all concerned because it embodies the elements of a true learning experience and utilizes most of them to the greatest extent possible. w

Regional Plan 2020

15.

Focusing on *Their* Future

I Teach: I Touch the Future.

So reads the familiar bumper sticker, and that is after all what we do. The children with whom we work are that future, and our job is to help them by providing them the opportunity to develop the real world skills they will need to make that future the best possible one for us all. By definition of this task, we teach to quality, not to facts. We shape attitudes, we model processes, we encourage behaviors that will affect the quality of life for our students and for ourselves as well. We get no grade for this, but the results will be obvious; life, after all, is outcome-based in the truest sense.

We get no grade for this, but the results will be obvious; life, after all, is outcome-based in the truest sense

Unfortunately, our traditional system of education does not always live up to this task. The very structure of that system too often detracts from rather than enhances the quality of our students' lives. The model provided by the conventional approach to education is woefully inadequate. In too many ways, schools are out of touch with the real world that exists beyond the classroom walls. Too many students enter school buildings each day hoping merely to survive the day, resigned to the boredom, the irrelevance, the isolation, and even the fear that pervades the hallways and the classrooms.

Is this the model we want for the future? Clearly, schools must be redesigned in both content and concept, in both medium and message if we are to change this model - and we *must* change this model. Whole-learning programs offer one possible solution. Whole-learning programs and activities such as those described here attempt to overcome the splintered experience offered by most curricula. In so doing, they reunify learning, revitalize it, and realign students' experiences with the real world.

In WATERSHED, our final learning activity of the year embodies this philosophy. We call the project "Regional Plan 2020," and it directly involves touching the future. The project requires students to use everything they have explored and learned in the past school year, including both informational content and process skills, to develop a regional plan for our area in the year 2020.

We choose 2020 for several reasons. First, there is the obvious reference to clear vision. Thanks to a television show of the same name, there is also a connotation with looking at things with a critical, analytical eye. More important, in the year 2020 our seventh grade students will be in their late thirties, full-fledged adults. They may well be sitting on planning commissions; we certainly hope they will be actively involved in their communities. The project, in this sense, is as real world as we can make it, and that world is *their* world.

In keeping with the whole-learning approach and its built-in emphasis on developing processes, this culminating activity is the most open-ended project of the year. It has the fewest delineated requirements and restrictions, and it allows students the greatest levels of control, as you can see from the following instruction sheet.

Students select their own groups and begin brainstorming. We circulate and play devil's advocate asking questions and raising issues for their consideration. When students require specific information, we steer them to the appropriate resource. This could be the library, or it could just as easily entail a phone call to a township official.

While this activity is going on, the class is also visiting energy, water, waste water, and solid waste treatment facilities. We compare these systems to those of the human body and of our homes.

We read and discuss articles concerning contemporary planning issues from the daily newspapers and periodicals – and there is never a dearth of such articles! We invite Adopt-a-Guest speakers (see Chapter 14) to visit us and share their expertise. We discuss environmental problems of both global and local concern, and students write their last American Diary to or from the future (see Chapter 8).

All the while, students continue to refine their visions of the region in 2020 and to prepare for their final major presentation of the year.

Needless to say, these final presentations can be both exciting and rewarding. Students eagerly share their visions and enthusiastically debate similarities and differences among group visions. In the course of doing so, many topics from the year's work resurface. Facts and concepts are reviewed and their interconnections reinforced.

When combined with the final self-evaluation, this learning activity ties the year together on many levels. Processes, products, skills, and information have merged and blended into an enjoyable and cohesive whole-learning model that students can carry with them as they continue their own journeys into the future. ш

REGIONAL PLAN 2020

As part of our look at the quality of life in our watersheds, we ask you to form a group of three or four to think about the future.

Start by drawing a good base map of the region that shows the streams and the fundamental topographical features. This map should be on poster board.

Now imagine that the year is 2020, twenty-two years from now. You and the others in your small group are now adults, and you are members of a regional planning commission. Your task is to determine what this area may be like based on what you have studied this year.

There are three major aspects you must cover, each of which can be shown on an acetate overlay attached to your base map.

- Population density and land use

- Transportation and communication systems

- Resources management systems/facilities for energy, water, waste water, and solid waste

During the last week of school, you will share your group's vision of the future with the rest of us. In addition to the maps, feel free to create any other visual aids which will enhance your presentation and make your vision clearer to the class. You might, for example, show us designs for housing in the future, or for transportation devices.

Remember, however, that you are not starting with a totally clean slate. You must think of what currently exists and forecast from that reality. Nevertheless, this is your chance to dream, to plan for the BEST possible future for our area, the place where YOUR children may one day grow up.

Now It's *Your* Turn! 16.

The fourteen learning activities described in this book represent a fraction of the opportunities provided in our whole-learning program. These activities allow students to experience the joy and excitement of true learning. You should realize that these activities are not carved in stone. They change every year, as they must, according to the needs and interests of our students. Feel free to take these ideas and adapt them to your own situation, but please try to do so in full awareness of the student-centered philosophy behind them.

As you implement these and related activities, keep in mind the five characteristics of a successful learning experience:

- a self-determined, highly personalized context that constitutes the motivation to learn

- an ongoing sense of personal control over the experience

- the opportunity to engage many of the senses and abilities

- a sense of enjoyment throughout the experience

- an awareness of achievement and potential application.

These characteristics have been consciously nurtured in the activities described; and, as you think about activities of your own, you should strive to incorporate them to the greatest extent possible. That is the basis of the whole-learning philosophy.

Once you adopt this philosophy, you will find ideas for new activities come easily, often from the students themselves. Furthermore, as you work more and more with this approach, you will come to see that the present structure of our educational system does not adequately meet the needs of our students. You will realize just how truly restrictive the traditional dis-

The present structure of our educational system does not meet the needs of our students.

ciplines and separated time period schedules are. You will become aware that the present system often stifles the very act of learning by denying students their true motivations to learn, by removing students' sense of control, and by negating the thrill and the joy inherent in real learning.

A harsh condemnation? Perhaps. Again I emphasize, that the system is to blame, not the teachers, per se. Teachers want to see their students experience true learning, but the system has become so entrenched and so stagnant over the past one hundred and fifty years that it no longer provides what our students truly need.

Yet the system remains intact. Why? Many teachers rely on the strength of tradition and thus fail to recognize the faults within the system. Of those who admit that problems exist, some believe that the system will not permit change. Frustrated, these teachers complain but do not act. Still others attempt to make small adjustments: a little cooperative learning here, an interdisciplinary unit there, oases in an academic desert. Perhaps you recognize yourself among these teachers. Perhaps you already feel the frustrations described. Perhaps you have already tried to implement some changes within the system.

To allow the system to remain unchanged, to perpetuate the system that prevents so many children from fulfilling their greater potential, is unconscionable.

As you work with the whole-learning philosophy, you will come to realize that all three of these avenues are dead ends. Even the oases turn out to be mirages. Tinkering with small, isolated changes within the existing system will never solve the problems. Minor modifications may, at best, provide temporary relief from some of the symptoms; at worst, they retard substantive change by masking the real problems that flaw the very heart of the system itself. Eventually, you will see the need for fundamental and substantive change that must be affected in a comprehensive, systemic manner. We need to reexamine the very idea and definition of curriculum, especially at the middle level. When you reach this conclusion, particularly after experiencing the advantages of a whole-learning approach, you may conclude that to allow the system to remain unchanged, to perpetuate the system that prevents so many children from fulfilling their greater potential, is unconscionable.

The important point to remember, however, is that you hold the key to change. We tell our **WATERSHED** students that knowledge must lead to action, and that the purpose for that action is to improve the quality of our life. The same holds true for you. You have seen the need for change; you have ideas for ways to improve the system. Armed with knowledge, you now assume the responsibility for putting that knowledge to use. To that end, I encourage you to try the whole-learning philosophy presented here.

Good luck, and let me know how you and your students fare. ɯ

National Middle School Association

National Middle School Association was established in 1973 to serve as a voice for professionals and others interested in the education of young adolescents. The association has grown rapidly and now enrolls members in all fifty states, the Canadian provinces, and forty-two other nations. In addition, fifty-six state, regional, and provincial middle school associations are official affiliates of NMSA.

NMSA is the only association dedicated exclusively to the education, development, and growth of young adolescents. Membership is open to all. While middle level teachers and administrators make up the bulk of the membership, central office personnel, college and university faculty, state department officials, other professionals, parents, and lay citizens are members and active in supporting our single mission – improving the educational experiences of 10-15 year olds. This open and diverse membership is a particular strength of NMSA.

The association provides a variety of services, conferences, and materials in fulfilling its mission. The association publishes *Middle School Journal*, the movement's premier professional journal; *Research in Middle Level Education Quarterly*; *Middle Ground, the Magazine of Middle Level Education; Target*, the association's newsletter; and *Family Connection*, a newsletter for families. In addition, the association publishes more than fifty books and monographs on all aspects of middle level education. The association's highly acclaimed annual conference, which has drawn approximately 10,000 registrants in recent years, is held in the fall.

For information about NMSA and its many services contact the headquarters at 2600 Corporate Exchange Drive, Suite 370, Columbus, Ohio 43231, TELEPHONE: 800-528-NMSA; FAX: 614-895-4750; www. NMSA.ORG.